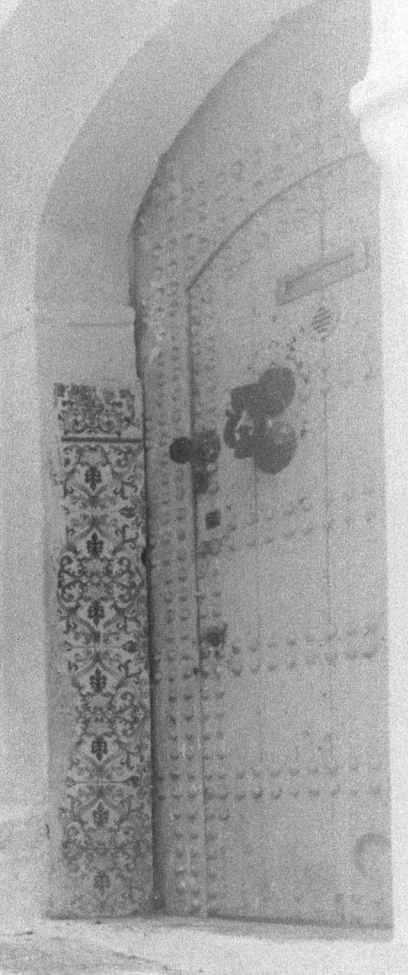

The Symphony of Resistance

The Symphony of Resistance

Bilingual Edition

selected poems of
Abdellatif Laâbi

translation and introduction by
Guillemette Johnston & Allan Johnston

SHANTI ARTS PUBLISHING
BRUNSWICK, MAINE

The Symphony of Resistance

Copyright © 2024 Abdellatif Laâbi (French)
Copyright © 2024 Guillemette Johnston and Allan Johnston (English)

All Rights Reserved
No part of this book may be used or reproduced in any manner whatsoever without the prior written permission of the publisher except for brief quotations in critical reviews.

Published by Shanti Arts Publishing
Interior and cover design by Shanti Arts Designs

Cover image: stockstudioX / istockphoto.com

Shanti Arts LLC
193 Hillside Road
Brunswick, Maine 04011

shantiarts.com

Printed in the United States of America

ISBN: 978-1-962082-16-7 (softcover)

Library of Congress Control Number: 2023952371

Contents

Acknowledgments 9

Introduction 13

    I.   The Shoulders and the Burden
          Les épaules et le fardeau 21

    II.   Vaccine
          Vaccin 61

    III. My Dear Double (i)
          Mon cher double (i) 65

    IV. Race
          Race 103

    V.   To My Son Yacine
          À mon fils Yacine 157

    VI. Four Years
          Quatre ans 165

    VII. The Signs Are There
          Les signes sont là 169

    VIII. The Poem Under Gag (i)
          Sous le bâillon le poème (i) 191

    IX. The Last Poem of Jean Sénac
          Le dernier poème de Jean Sénac 203

    X.   Pastures of Silence
          Pâturages du silence 211

    XI. Flayed Alive—Epilogue
          L'écorché vif—Épilogue 255

    XII. Poems Fallen from the Train
          Poèmes tombés du train 259

Contributors 291

Acknowledgments

Les épaules et le fardeau : from *Tribulations d'un rêveur attitré*. Paris : Clepsydre/Éditions de la différence, 2008; Rabat : Éditions Marsam, 2009, p. 33–52.

Vaccin : from *Tribulations d'un rêveur attitré*. Paris : Clepsydre/Éditions de la différence, 2008; Rabat : Éditions Marsam, 2009, p. 146–147.

Mon cher double (I) : from *Mon cher double*. Paris : Clepsydre/Éditions de la différence, 2007, p. 9–28.

Race : from *Œuvre poétique I*. Paris : Éditions de la différence, 2006, p. 69-91. From *Le règne de barbarie* (1965–1967).

À mon fils Yacine : from *Œuvre poétique I*. Paris : Éditions de la différence, 2006, p. 120–122.

Quatre ans : from *Œuvre poétique I*. Paris : Éditions de la différence, 2006, p. 180–181.

Les signes sont là : from *Écris la vie*. Paris : Éditions de la différence, 2005, p. 37–60.

Sous le bâillon le poème : from *Œuvre poétique I*. Paris : Éditions de la différence, 2006, p. 231–237.

Le dernier poème de Jean Sénac : from *Œuvre poétique I*. Paris : Éditions de la différence, 2006, p. 365–370.

Pâturages du silence : from *Discours sur la colline Arabe*. Paris : Éditions L'Harmattan, 1985, p. 35–84 ; *Œuvre poétique I*. Paris : Éditions de la différence, 2006, p. 287–308.

L'écorché vif—Épilogue : from *Œuvre poétique I*. Paris : Éditions de la différence, 2006, p. 337.

Poèmes tombés du train : from *Tous les déchirements*. Paris : Messidor, 1990, p. 87–104 ; *Œuvre poétique I*. Paris : Éditions de la différence, 2006, p. 407–422.

Some of these translations have previously been published in the following journals, sometimes in altered form:

AzonaL: "Flayed Alive—Epilogue"; "The Last Poem of Jean Sénac"; and "The Signs Are There"

Ezra: "The Shoulders and the Burden" (earlier version of the last stanza) and "Vaccine"

MayDay Magazine: "The Poem Under Gag"

Metamorphoses: "Four Years"; "Race"; and "To My Son Yacine"

Transference: "My Dear Double" and "The Shoulders and the Burden" (published with commentary)

"So Much Light Around Me"

An Introduction to
The Symphony of Resistance,
a Selection of Poems by Abdellatif Laâbi

Guillemette and Allan Johnston

A celebration of surviving, resisting, and standing as witness lies at the heart of many of the poems in this selection of works by the great Moroccan poet Abdellatif Laâbi. Surviving, as Laâbi tells us, is living, living is freedom, and freedom is, or at least is akin to, poetry:

> The poem
> if it is a poem
> will always astonish
> —that's the least of things—
> It is the same with its sister
> liberty

The twelve poems and sequences included in this volume come again and again to moments of confrontation with the forces of an unjust world, moments that ask us to exist in and in some ways alongside or outside that world. "The Shoulders and the Burden," the first poem of the collection, offers intense, telegraphic representations of catastrophic scenes reflecting the disasters besetting post-colonial societies. Laâbi considers the burden—and anguish—that comes with knowing the limits we face when confronting such vehement violence, exploitation, and abuse. Living in such a world without retreating into utter depression, televised fantasy, or breast-beating fanaticism seems increasingly difficult. But Laâbi takes this moment to define the near-sacred role of the witness that belongs to the poet, requiring that one remain a "man of his word":

> You will be guardian and vestal virgin
> of the speck of light
> dispensed to your species
> sunken into your guts
> With these prerequisites
> you will merit your true name
> man of his word
> or poet if you wish

Laâbi has authored numerous poetry collections as well as novels, essays, autobiographies, children's books, and other works, and has translated important literary works and authors into French to expand knowledge of Maghreb and Arabic culture. In the 1960s he cofounded the journal *Souffles-Anfas*, a major vehicle for the dissemination of literature and ideas in the newly liberated countries of the post-colonial period. As a result of his role in founding this journal as well as his political activism, Laâbi ended up spending more than eight years in Moroccan prisons for "crimes of opinion." Released in 1980, he has lived since 1985 in France, where he continues to write and to support issues pertaining to human rights, particularly in relation to the Arabic world. As he puts it, "Everything which the Arab reality offers that is generous, open and creative is crushed by regimes whose only anxiety is to perpetuate their own power and self-serving interest. And what is often worse is to see that the West remains insensitive to the daily tragedy while at the same time accommodating, not to say supporting, the ruling classes who strangle the free will and aspirations of their people."

The poems in this collection offer a broad perspective on Laâbi's poetic works. They include pieces that reflect on his time in prison, address the impact of post-colonialism on politics and identity, and explore the fate of the poet in the modern world. "Vaccine," for instance, describes a scene at Orly airport in Paris where Laâbi's bag comes out worse for wear due to inspection, an experience that makes him think he "shaved [his] beard just in time" and ponder the possibility of inventing a strong remedy to prejudice, a "horse vaccine / against triumphant stupidity." In "My Dear Double" Laâbi describes a second self, an uncanny doppelgänger that often machinates against his wishes, causing a second seeing, one that leads him to the challenge of battle with himself, just as the toreador at the end of the poem turns to face and entice the bull. Doubling here is a problematic yet ultimately empowering force. "Race," a cry of release of the self from the pressures of post-colonial identity that Pierre Joris compares to Allen Ginsberg's "Howl," offers a frenetic flipping between scatterings of poetic lines and blocks of textual scraps jammed together, creating a cry of desperation that is answered by an appeal to the famous Egyptian singer Oum Kalthoum, a matriarchal force allowing affirmation of the possible realization of the body as the ground for a "first epic"—the epic that in fact is the poem that has just been read. Such vast leaps in Laâbi's imagination and style speak to the richness of the sensibility behind the poems, a quality Khalid Lyamlahy emphasizes when he mentions the "contrast between quietness and violence, elegance and resistance, love and revolt" that "is one of the most central features of Laâbi's poetry."

Many of these poems reflect upon Laâbi's years of imprisonment, a traumatizing experience that has left its mark on the poet. "To My Son Yacine" responds to a letter he received from his son while in prison, while "Four Years" recalls family visits of "a quarter hour a week / through two gates separated by a corridor." "The Signs Are There" addresses the lingering effects of this experience. Toward the end of the poem Laâbi speaks of those who suffered from and resisted such intimidation, those for whom

> [e]very smile
> has the value and weight
> of overwhelming experienced pain

> Of cries never uttered
> to disappoint the torturers

Through resistance, those who have survived can now look back on the ordeals they endured and celebrate the life they earned or kept with difficulty in spite of their suffering. Bringing out the quality of intimacy and oral sharing that is so central to his poetic accomplishment, Laâbi acknowledges the pain he and fellow prisoners of conscience experienced, raising the voices of the sufferers in ways that only survivors can fully relate to. This world of spoken intimacy is witnessed in the simple, oral quality of Laâbi's voice throughout these poems:

> Among so many victories
> ugly and stupefying
> the one
> so rare
> of the vanquished
> is and ought to be modest
> It is with a few friends
> that it is usually celebrated
> on fleeting occasions
> where the actors who are now
> witnesses embrace
> slap each other roughly on the back
> double over with laughter at the deliverance
> and end up raising a glass

"The Poem Under Gag" again explores the harshness of prison, while "The Last Poem of Jean Sénac" eulogizes the famous *pied-noir* Algerian nationalist poet who was murdered in 1973 at the age of forty-eight—a crime that to this day remains unsolved. "Pastures of Silence" again looks back to the prison experience, linking the time lost in incarceration to creativity in its recognition that

> Nothing in the world
> will oblige you
> to surrender
> to renounce
> your human identity

"Epilogue—Flayed Alive" questions that link as it witnesses the slow disintegration of the Arab poet, while "Poems Fallen from the Train" gathers observation and musings such as one might have while commuting and gazing vacantly out the window.

• • •

Just as in the conjunction of multiple sounds that generate a symphonic performance, the poems in this volume offer the reader a lasting song of resistance celebrated through Laâbi's evocative writing. What makes Laâbi's poetry unique and original in French are the subtle interactions of multidimensional influences emanating from two different languages that have merged in Laâbi's own idiosyncratic style, where idioms, rhythms, and sounds converge within the medium of his poetry. Arabic and French inhabit Laâbi's mind, his past, and his present, and provide the key to the heart of his talent. As he puts it, "my birth-language is Arabic, my writing language is French. Perhaps what makes what I write unique is that the two cultures are intertwined. Even when I am writing in French, my Arabic language is there. There is a musicality in Arabic, and these words enter into my French texts."

This sense of the dual quality of Laâbi's language expresses itself in ways that transcend the textual, insofar as Laâbi links it to "a new kind of literature . . . currently emerging" in what he would call "the peripheries of the world—India, Africa, or elsewhere." This new kind of literature straddles "two cultures, two imaginations, and two different languages." Mohammed Belmaïzi describes it thus:

Laâbi has forged a twofold textual type of writing, where orality has a preponderant role. In Laâbi's work, the written French, for which the Latin alphabet is used, is molded through orality. That means that each French word, said out loud, is going to create another word that provides the sonorous image of the Arabic language. Thus, there are two overlapping texts: a written one and an oral one; whatever is said in French will be heard in Arabic.

The effects of this duality in Laâbi's writing can arguably be said to go beyond the realm of oral quality as it is manifested in the written text. The second self in "My Dear Double" interferes in his life, presenting an alternate perspective. This uncanny sense of viewing oneself as the other brings us back to the role of witness, the primary function of the onlooker who simultaneously experiences and stands outside of events, testifying to their occurrence. Whether this spectator attests to the horrors of prison, the savagery of the world, or even just whatever one passes by while riding the train, he assumes the role of verifier; he is there as a reporting witness, either poet or guardian of the special light. As long as there is a standing witness, the light remains.

I

The Shoulders and the Burden

Les épaules et le fardeau

The Shoulders and the Burden

By itself
the gate gave way
The invitation is polite
and firm
A few short steps
and the world comes again
just as it is
with familiar shipwrecks
As an eyewitness
submerged to the neck
you will have to stretch yourself
even more
Will your heart hold?

Les épaules et le fardeau

De lui-même
le portail a cédé
L'invitation est courtoise
et ferme
À peine quelques enjambées
et le monde se présente à nouveau
tel qu'il est
familier des naufrages
Témoin oculaire
noyé jusqu'au cou
tu vas devoir tirer encore plus
sur la corde
Le cœur tiendra-t-il ?

Vertigo from standing
holding a vague helm
Frail is the boat
The reefs redoubtable
The prayer words forgotten
The anchor
will not be thrown
from heaven

Vertige d'être debout
tenant un vague gouvernail
Frêle est l'embarcation
Redoutables les récifs
Oubliés les mots de la prière
L'ancre
ne sera pas jetée
du ciel

If only an azure gap
the piercing of a hardened star
speaking
before the obligatory meeting
with twilight
How easy it would be
to nourish
the horses of reason
straight from
the manger of clouds

Si seulement une trouée d'azur
la percée d'une étoile aguerrie
parlante
avant le rendez-vous obligé
du crépuscule
Comme il serait aisé
de nourrir
les chevaux de la raison
à même
la mangeoire des nuages

The earth
flat or round
What's the difference?
if we must inevitably
retrace our steps
and find nothing
but collapsed bridges
carcasses of houses
where crows have made nest
profaned gardens and graves
concrete arch from whose mast
the same flag hangs half-mast
and no living soul
to recount without adding
the thousandth episode
of this pitiful apocalypse

La terre
plate ou ronde
Quelle différence ?
si l'on doit immanquablement
revenir sur ses pas
et ne trouver
que ponts écroulés
carcasses de maisons
où le corbeau a fait son nid
jardins et tombes profanés
arche en béton au mât de laquelle
pend le même drapeau en berne
et pas âme qui vive
pour narrer sans en rajouter
le millième épisode
de cette piètre apocalypse

The human-inhuman beast
more and more intelligent
still using
old worn out ruses
such as this one-way path
to salvation
where today bulldozers carve
the highway of a civilization
as basic
as the hamburger
that serves as its mascot
And enslaved people
scrambling to the gate
with perfect awareness
and last-ditch despair

La bête humaine-inhumaine
de plus en plus intelligente
usant encore
de vieilles ruses éventées
telle cette voie unique
du salut
où des bulldozers tracent aujourd'hui
l'autoroute d'une civilisation
aussi sommaire
que le hamburger
qui lui sert de mascotte
Et les peuples asservis
de se bousculer au portillon
en parfaite connaissance
et désespoir de cause

As if one could choose
from the range of horror
covering the planet
Reason wavers
but we must recover
Be indignant
denounce
certainly
For all that
will our debt be paid?
Anger cools down
while other raging fires
present themselves
to the permanence of horror

Comme si l'on pouvait choisir
dans l'éventail de l'horreur
couvrant la planète
La raison vacille
mais il faut se reprendre
S'indigner
dénoncer
certes
Pour autant
serons-nous quittes ?
La colère se refroidit
tandis que d'autres brasiers
se présentent
à la permanence de l'horreur

At dinner time
images announced as unbearable
We look away
no longer knowing what distinguishes
decency from indecency
and when we look
the line is just as thin
between cowardice and courage
At the end of the meal
We sometimes wonder
if we have not eaten
the flesh of our neighbor
more precisely
that of our own children
The soccer match
or the primetime movie
comes just in time
to sweep away these little worries

À l'heure de dîner
les images annoncées comme insoutenables
On détourne les yeux
ne sachant plus ce qui distingue
la décence de l'indécence
et quand on regarde
la ligne est tout aussi mince
entre lâcheté et courage
À la fin du repas
il arrive qu'on se demande
si l'on n'a pas mangé
la chair de son prochain
plus précisément
celle de ses propres enfants
Le match de foot
ou le film en prime time
vient à point nommé
balayer ces petits soucis

Hell is well stocked
but the shelves
are empty
except for the ever more
sophisticated cameras
The tours are led
by scholars in uniform
and ethnicolor headwear
"In the name of God" proclaims one
"What you must know" warns the other
and all start singing the same war cry
"Get thee behind me, Satan!"
Modern hell
has a damn good advantage
over its predecessors
It is shot in a studio

L'enfer est bien achalandé
mais ses rayons d'approvisionnement
sont vides
sauf de caméras
de plus en plus sophistiquées
Les visites sont commentées
par des savants portant uniforme
et couvre-chefs ethnicolor
« Au nom de Dieu », proclame l'un
« Ce qu'il faut savoir », avertit l'autre
et tous d'entonner le même cri de guerre
« Arrière Satan ! »
L'enfer moderne
possède un sacré avantage
sur les précédents
Il est tourné en studio

Unlike all the messages
constantly drummed in
on compassion, justice
hope, love
the wrath of heaven descends first
—let it be said in passing—
on the convicts of existence
the helpless ones
without teeth and shoulders
And the ones whose hearts cannot hear
the narrow-minded in spirit
the toothy ambitious grave diggers
with faces completely remade
barking in the face of the survivors
and right in the ear of the dead:
Atone for your sins!

Contrairement à tous les messages
rabâchés
sur la compassion, la justice
l'espérance, l'amour
la colère du ciel s'abat en priorité
—soit dit en passant—
sur les condamnés de l'existence
les désemparés
sans dents et sans épaules
Et les malentendants du cœur
les borgnes de l'esprit
les fossoyeurs aux dents longues
au visage entièrement refait
d'aboyer à la face des survivants
et jusqu'à l'oreille des trépassés :
Expiez vos péchés !

From one disaster to the next
immutable scenario
Help is slow
eventually arrives
The neediest
are the last ones served
Scraps as usual

D'une catastrophe l'autre
scénario immuable
Les secours tardent
finissent par arriver
Les plus démunis
sont les derniers servis
Des rogatons comme d'habitude

Note to illegals:
with those poorer than they are
the poor
can be pitiless
They have that at least in common
with the rich bastards

Avis aux clandestins :
avec plus pauvres qu'eux
les pauvres
peuvent être impitoyables
Ils ont au moins cela en commun
avec les salopards de riches

How beautiful she is
today's Africa!
It was yesterday
—and it already seems unreal—
that we celebrated the wedding
of her newfound freedom
and the bride
more desirable than in our dreams
"dressed in her color that is life"
insolently young
exhibiting her flower and heated breasts
leading the trance
that gives soul to the body
light to the eyes
inspired words to lips
the nigger finally standing
united in the recognition of blood
the only approved human color
That was yesterday
orphaned day
of an aborted genesis

Elle est bien belle
l'Afrique d'aujourd'hui !
C'était hier
—et c'est déjà irréel—
que nous avons célébré les noces
de sa liberté retrouvée
et l'épousée
encore plus désirable que dans nos rêves
« vêtue de sa couleur qui est vie »
insolemment jeune
exhibant sa fleur et ses seins d'ardeur
conduisant la transe
qui rend l'âme au corps
la lumière aux yeux
la parole inspirée à la bouche
Sa négraille enfin debout
unie dans la reconnaissance du sang
seule couleur agréée de l'homme
C'était hier
jour orphelin
d'une genèse avortée

Africa!
Your pariah peoples
withered limbs of the primary stump
conceived in your alluvial silt
Your errant peoples
in the frozen furnace of an enclosure
with the dimension of the continent
Your blinded peoples
harnessed
bending under the yoke
turning the wheel
that crushes
the fruits of their womb
The envious
who insidiously praised your youth
have condemned you to die young
The announced extinction of the species
will commence with you

Africa !
Tes peuples parias
rameaux rabougris de la souche originelle
conçue dans ton limon
Tes peuples errants
dans la fournaise glacée d'un enclos
à la dimension du Continent
Tes peuples aveuglés
attelés
ployant sous le joug
faisant tourner la meule
qui écrase
les fruits de leurs entrailles
Les envieux
qui vantaient insidieusement ta jeunesse
t'ont condamnée à mourir jeune
L'extinction annoncée de l'espèce
commencera par toi

Under so much abuse
the vessel of memory
risks overflowing
and besides no one knows
if its bottom is watertight
Should it be warmed up gently
or left to cool?
The soup of crime
naturally abundant
is more widely distributed
than soup from soup kitchens
It often sits in the stomach
and can cause nausea
but its vapors
numb consciences
cyclically

À force de sévices
le récipient de la mémoire
risque de déborder
et l'on ne sait d'ailleurs
si le fond en est étanche
Faut-il réchauffer à feu doux
ou laisser refroidir ?
La soupe du crime
naturellement abondante
est plus largement distribuée
que la soupe populaire
Elle reste souvent sur l'estomac
et provoque des nausées
mais ses vapeurs engourdissent
cycliquement
les consciences

The list cannot be exhaustive
There are children tossed aside
for the scavengers of sex and war
the blackmail of famine
the dealing in despair
the organ trafficking of thought
the white-washing of filthy ideas
There is the abduction of rebels
who raised their hand to the Temple
the crushing of the least bud
that had the idea to open
in memory of dead hope
There is the perfect crime
the immunity of Power
knighted and hailed at the Stock Exchange
There are the glasses they clink
the decent smutty ones
and the laughing of the winners
two steps from the mass graves

La liste ne saurait être exhaustive
Il y a les enfants jetés en pâture
aux charognards du sexe et de la guerre
le chantage à la famine
le négoce du désespoir
le trafic d'organes de la pensée
le blanchiment des idées sales
Il y a le rapt des rebelles
ayant levé la main sur le Temple
l'écrasement du moindre bourgeon
qui a eu l'idée d'éclore
en souvenir de la défunte espérance
Il y a le crime parfait
l'immunité de la Force
adoubée et acclamée à la Bourse
Il y a les verres qu'on entrechoque
les propres graveleux
et le rire des vainqueurs
à deux pas des charniers

Knowledge is unforgiving
It gnaws at you
Of what would you be guilty?
Of some omission
or of having gone too far
Of feeling yourself burning with the words
that you gave to the unspeakable
and staying screwed down to your seat
while sipping your coffee?
Just say it:
even innocent of evil
you are its hostage
Can one pacify the hearts of executioners
change humanity?
No one has the answer
Redemption, Redemption
you murmur
that unsolvable equation

La connaissance ne pardonne pas
Elle te ronge
De quoi serais-tu coupable ?
D'un quelconque oubli
ou de surenchère
De te sentir brûler avec les mots
que tu as mis sur l'innommable
et de rester vissé sur ton siège
en sirotant ton café ?
Ose le dire :
même innocent du mal
tu en es l'otage
Peut-on pacifier le cœur des bourreaux
changer d'humanité ?
Personne n'a la réponse
La rédemption, la Rédemption
murmures-tu
cette équation insoluble

Let us not talk about the tyrants
who lately sought to impose on you
the law of silence
nor of the small-time dictators
peddlers of renown
only lending to the rich
at the cost of revenge
More unworthy are the cultists
of an immaculate poetry
who not only keep silent
or prevaricate
but who would like
to gag you
at the first opportunity

Ne parlons pas des tyrans
qui ont cherché naguère à t'imposer
la loi du silence
ni des petits satrapes de l'heure
colporteurs de la renommée
ne prêtant qu'aux riches
à charge de revanche
Plus indignes sont les sectateurs
d'une poésie immaculée
qui non seulement se taisent
ou biaisent
mais voudraient bien
te bâillonner
à la première occasion

No matter what happens
you will use your right of insurrection
You will acquit yourself
with an open face
of the duty to discern
unveil
lacerate
each face of abjection
You will be guardian and vestal virgin
of the speck of light
dispensed to your species
sunken into your guts
With these prerequisites
you will merit your true name
man of his word
or poet if you wish

Du droit de t'insurger tu useras
quoi qu'il advienne
Du devoir de discerner
dévoiler
lacérer
chaque visage de l'abjection
tu t'acquitteras
à visage découvert
De la graine de lumière
dispensée à ton espèce
chue dans tes entrailles
tu te feras gardien et vestale
À ces conditions préalables
tu mériteras ton vrai nom
homme de parole
ou poète si l'on veut

It is not a matter of shoulders
or of biceps
the burden of the world
Those who have come to carry it
are often the most frail
They too are subject to fear
to doubt
to discouragement
and sometimes end up cursing
the splendid Idea or Dream
that has exposed them
to the fires of Gehenna
But if they bend
they do not break
and when by frequent misery
they are cut and mutilated
these human reeds
know that their bodies
lacerated by betrayal
will become so many flutes
the shepherds of awakening will play
to capture
and convey to the stars
the symphony of resistance

Ce n'est pas une affaire d'épaules
ni de biceps
que le fardeau du monde
Ceux qui viennent à le porter
sont souvent les plus frêles
Eux aussi sont sujets à la peur
au doute
au découragement
et en arrivent parfois à maudire
l'Idée ou le Rêve splendides
qui les ont exposés
au feu de la géhenne
Mais s'ils plient
ils ne rompent pas
et quand par malheur fréquent
on les coupe et mutile
ces roseaux humains
savent que leurs corps lardés
par la traîtrise
deviendront autant de flûtes
que des bergers de l'éveil emboucheront
pour capter
et convoyer jusqu'aux étoiles
la symphonie de la résistance

II

Vaccine

Vaccin

Vaccine

Paris Orly
You have front row seats
at the baggage belt
watching for the red suit case
you broke in with this epic journey
When it comes out after a long wait
you can hardly recognize it
One would think it had passed
through the bowels of a coal mine
Also it is falling to pieces
What inquisitor pleased himself
by visiting it so rudely
when you had put your poems
in the shelter of your carry-on?
Come on, stop your drama
look at it this way
today's inquisition puts on gloves
and uses x-rays
It has other worries in mind
You shaved your beard just in time
and no longer think the revolution
is coming tomorrow
The day after perhaps, if you
succeed in perfecting
in your secret laboratory
a horse vaccine
against triumphant stupidity

Vaccin

Paris Orly
Tu es aux premières loges
du tapis roulant
à guetter la valise rouge
que tu as étrennée pendant ce périple
Quand elle sort après longue attente
tu as de la peine à la reconnaître
On dirait qu'elle a traversé
les boyaux d'une mine de charbon
De plus elle est toute déglinguée
Quel inquisiteur s'est plu
à la visiter sans aménité
alors que tu avais mis tes poèmes
à l'abri dans ton bagage à main ?
Allons, arrête ton cinéma
te ravises-tu
l'inquisition d'aujourd'hui enfile des gants
et utilise les rayons
Elle a d'autres martels en tête
Toi, tu t'es rasé la barbe à temps
et ne penses plus que la révolution
est pour demain
Après-demain peut-être, si tu réussis
à mettre au point
dans ton laboratoire secret
un vaccin de cheval
contre la bêtise triomphante

III

My Dear Double (i)

Mon cher double (i)

My Dear Double

My double
an old acquaintance
whom I visit with moderation
He is a shameless one
who plays on my timidity
and knows how to take advantage
of my distractions
He is the shadow
that follows or precedes me
aping my gait
He sneaks into my dreams
and fluently speaks
the language of my demons
Despite our great intimacy
he remains a stranger to me
I neither hate nor love him
for after all
he is my double
the proof by default
of my existence

Mon cher double

Mon double
une vieille connaissance
que je fréquente avec modération
C'est un sans-gêne
qui joue de ma timidité
et sait mettre à profit
mes distractions
Il est l'ombre
qui me suit ou me précède
en singeant ma démarche
Il s'immisce jusque dans mes rêves
et parle couramment
la langue de mes démons
Malgré notre grande intimité
il me reste étranger
Je ne le hais ni ne l'aime
car après tout
il est mon double
la preuve par défaut
de mon existence

Sometimes
I find him sitting in my place
and don't dare ask him
to get up
I recognize him by the particular odor
of my finger joints
when I am not well
His carnal inconsistence
troubles me
and I'm a little jealous of it
Since there is only one seat
in my bedroom
I stay standing
I imagine that he works for me
in his own way
He paints on the light
to show me
how I should go about it
with words
and if I decide to open my mouth
he suddenly disappears

Parfois
je le trouve assis à ma place
et n'ose pas lui dire
de se lever
Je le reconnais à l'odeur particulière
de mes phalanges
quand je suis souffrant
Son inconsistance charnelle
me trouble
et j'en suis un peu jaloux
Comme il n'y a qu'un siège
dans la chambre
je reste debout
J'imagine qu'il travaille pour moi
à sa façon
Il peint sur la lumière
pour m'indiquer
comment je dois m'y prendre
avec les mots
et si je m'avise d'ouvrir la bouche
aussitôt il disparaît

When I look at the sea
ignoring the waves
he turns his back to me
—in a manner of speaking—
It seems like he is listening
to the sound of a secret clock
marking off the part
of time allotted to death
When I raise my eyes
from the sea
to the swelling peak
he persists in seeing nothing
but the abyss
He spoils my fun
with his pretentions
to lucidity

Quand je regarde la mer
en faisant abstraction des vagues
lui me tourne le dos
—façon de parler—
On dirait qu'il prête l'oreille
au bruit d'une horloge secrète
égrenant du temps
la part dévolue à la mort
De la mer
que je soulève des yeux
et porte à la cime
il s'obstine à ne scruter
que l'abîme
Il me gâche mon plaisir
avec ses prétentions
à la lucidité

As soon
as I discover a country
he surveys another one
and sends me derogatory messages
What amazes me
leaves him stone cold
The language I introduce myself to
does not have the caliber
of the one he sputters
The national dish
I'm about to savor
without preconception
always lacks the spice
or the creaminess he adores
and in the beauty
that bowls me over in passing
he inevitably seeks and finds
the hidden defect
That's why for some time
I have limited
my voyages

Au moment
où je découvre un pays
il en arpente un autre
et m'envoie des messages désobligeants
Ce qui m'émerveille
le laisse de marbre
La langue à laquelle je m'initie
n'atteint pas la cheville
de celle qu'il bredouille
Le plat national
que je m'apprête à déguster
sans préjugé
manque toujours du piquant
ou de l'onctueux dont il raffole
et de la beauté
qui me renverse au passage
il cherche et trouve immanquablement
le vice caché
Voilà pourquoi je limite
depuis quelque temps
mes voyages

He whispers to me
that he's holding back
the word I have
on the tip of my tongue
for my own good
If I have become a real master
of hindsight
to whom do I owe it
If I walk with purpose
who decides?
Ah I strongly doubt
my solitude
when I talk to myself
It may be
that it's only when I kiss
that I completely feel
myself

Le mot que j'ai
sur le bout de la langue
c'est lui qui le retient
pour mon bien
me souffle-t-il
Si je suis passé maître
en esprit d'escalier
à qui le dois-je
Si je marche d'un pas décidé
qui en décide ?
Ah je doute fort
de ma solitude
quand je parle tout seul
A la rigueur
ce n'est que lorsque j'embrasse
que je me sens entièrement
moi-même

At the turn of a phrase
of a strophe
I stumble upon words
it would never cross my mind
to use
on hackneyed images
reminiscences of the stone age
of thought
I get alarmed
The artisan I am
suspects some talent
for snake-like deceit
I'm not ready to swallow
I thus deal
with a forewarned bird-catcher
a cultivated censor
a fine craftsman of doublespeak
"Know thyself," the wise one asserted
Certainly
but things being what they are
I would like to add:
Beware of that self

Au détour d'une phrase
d'une strophe
je tombe sur des vocables
qu'il ne me viendrait pas à l'idée
d'utiliser
sur des images éculées
des réminiscences de l'âge de pierre
de la pensée
Je m'alarme
L'artisan que je suis
soupçonne quelque industrie
des couleuvres
que je ne suis pas prêt à avaler
J'ai donc affaire
à un oiseleur averti
un censeur cultivé
un fin tailleur de langue de bois
« Connais-toi toi-même », affirmait le sage
Certes
mais les choses étant ce qu'elles sont
il me faudrait ajouter :
Méfie-toi de ce moi-là

He claims to be Argentinian
while I have a hard time
considering myself French
You would die more Moroccan than he is
while I revel
in my savage freedom
of statelessness
He argues
in favor of cremation
and me I am far
from having solved
the riddle of where
to be buried
He tries to enroll
in tango classes
without respect
for my fully screwed up
spinal column
To say the least
he exhausts me

Lui se prétend argentin
alors que j'ai du mal
à m'estimer français
Plus marocain que lui tu meurs
quand je me complais
dans ma sauvage liberté
d'apatride
Il argumente
en faveur de la crémation
et moi je suis loin
d'avoir réglé
le casse-tête d'une terre
de sépulture
Il cherche à s'inscrire
à des cours de tango
sans égard
pour ma colonne vertébrale
largement foutue
C'est peu de dire
qu'il m'épuise

Take risks
Make an effort?
It's not his cup of tea
For me it's the roller coaster
the pass of Thermopylae
Charybdis and Scylla
the Augean stables
the torment of Tantalus
the throes
of the Iraqi quagmire
the Gaza powder-keg
and the voyages Sinbad
has not dared to tell
I am the overflow
of his fears
the factotum
of his grand ideas
And the worst
is that I put up with it
without flinching

Prendre des risques
Se mouiller la chemise ?
Ce n'est ne pas sa tasse de thé
À moi les montagnes russes
le défilé des Thermopyles
Charybde et Scylla
les écuries d'Augias
le supplice de Tantale
les affres
du bourbier de l'Irak
de la poudrière de Gaza
et les voyages que Sindbad
n'a pas osé raconter
Je suis le déversoir
de ses frayeurs
le factotum
de ses grandes idées
Et le pire
c'est que j'encaisse
sans broncher

I would have liked
at my venerable age
to quietly cultivate my garden
caress the leaves of my bamboo
and polish them one by one
play the bee to my roses
and gather my fill of nectar
bury my arms in the earth
and patiently wait until they grow back
as two magnolias
and thus stretch out my branches
to collect the dew of the firmament
shelter the migratory birds
or children
who would have read and appreciated
The Baron in the Trees
No
it's no good
when I hear the snickering
of the one who persists
in planting around me
a hedge
of deforming mirrors

J'aurais bien aimé
à mon âge respectable
cultiver tranquillement mon jardin
caresser les feuilles de mon bambou
et les lustrer une à une
me faire l'abeille de mes roses
et les butiner à satiété
enfoncer mes bras dans la terre
et attendre patiemment qu'ils repoussent
en deux magnolias
tendre ainsi mes branches
pour recueillir la rosée du firmament
abriter les oiseaux migrateurs
ou les enfants
qui auraient lu et apprécié
Le Baron perché
Non
rien à faire
quand j'entends les ricanements
de celui qui s'acharne
à planter autour de moi
une haie
de miroirs déformants

One day
inspired by Abraham's story
on official assignment
I get ready to slit the intruder's throat
hoping
it goes without saying
for divine intervention
in the form of a ram
or lacking that
a turkey
Seeing nothing coming
and getting desperate
I resolve
to turn the weapon on myself
What weapon?
I only see between my fingers
an ordinary Bic pen
and am enraged to discover
it has dried up

Un jour
m'inspirant de l'histoire d'Abraham
en service commandé
je m'apprête à égorger l'intrus
en espérant
cela va sans dire
l'intervention divine
sous forme de bélier
ou à défaut
de dindon
Ne voyant rien venir
et en désespoir de cause
je me résous
à retourner l'arme contre moi
Quelle arme ?
Je ne vois entre mes doigts
qu'un stylo Bic ordinaire
et j'enrage en découvrant
qu'il vient de rendre l'âme

I also sometimes happen to reason
to myself saying:
Let us accept this division of tasks
One lookout is not enough
there should be two, ten, a thousand
And then
what is the external voice
without the inner one
weighing carefully
each thing and its opposite
listening to
the most distant memory
the labyrinth's familiar
guiding us thus
toward accuracy of expression
and comprehensive vision
placing on our tongue
oh so rarely
the melting seed of reconciliation
with ourselves

Il m'arrive aussi de me raisonner
en me disant :
Acceptons cette division des tâches
Une vigie ne suffit pas
il en faudrait deux, dix, mille
Et puis
qu'est la voix extérieure
sans celle du dedans
pesant scrupuleusement
la chose et son contraire
à l'écoute de la mémoire
la plus lointaine
familière du labyrinthe
nous guidant ainsi
vers le juste de l'expression
et le large de la vision
déposant sur notre langue
oh si rarement
la graine fondante de la réconciliation
avec nous-même

Without warning
he disappears for a long time
to the point that I start
to doubt
his existence
Like a troubled soul
I feel less useful
than an onion skin
Aridity overcomes me
My inner voice
is only a gurgle
and my being
is reduced to a gut
So
I spread myself on my bed
and close my eyes
cursing poets
and poetry

Sans crier gare
il advient qu'il disparaisse longuement
au point que je commence
à douter
de son existence
Comme une âme en peine
je me sens moins utile
qu'une pelure d'oignon
L'aridité me gagne
Ma voix intérieure
n'est plus qu'un gargouillis
et mon être là
en est réduit à un tube digestif
Alors
je m'étale sur mon lit
et ferme les yeux
en maudissant les poètes
et la poésie

Is he the despot
or is it me
The empire we are fighting over
is it worth it
Does it truly exist
or is it only a mirage
formed by the vapors of drunkenness
and the chilled steam
of compassion
Is it a haven
Or a trap door?
Poor him
poor me
who play hopscotch
with the bigger kids
pretending to forget
that the guardians of prosperity
also shoot at the old
even if they still
have children's eyes

Est-ce lui le despote
ou est-ce moi
L'empire que l'on se dispute
en vaut-il la chandelle
Existe-t-il vraiment
ou n'est-ce que mirage
formé par les vapeurs des cuites
et la buée refroidie
de la compassion
Est-ce un havre
ou une trappe ?
Pauvre de lui
pauvre de moi
qui jouons à la marelle
dans la cour des grands
feignant d'oublier
que les gardiens de la prospérité
tirent aussi sur les vieillards
même s'ils ont gardé
leurs yeux d'enfants

Have I invented him
for the sake of the cause?
I assure you no
I can still distinguish
a white thread
from a black thread
the breathing of stone
from the hot breath of living spirit
I am rarely wrong
about the origin of fragrances
the density of air
the nature of prints
left in the sand
on the skin
or the retina
Don't worry
I have not yet crossed
the fine line

L'ai-je inventé
pour les besoins de la cause ?
Je vous assure que non
Je sais encore distinguer
un fil blanc
d'un fil noir
la respiration de la pierre
du souffle chaud de l'esprit vivant
Je me trompe rarement
sur l'origine des parfums
la densité de l'air
la nature des empreintes
laissées sur le sable
la peau
ou la rétine
Rassurez-vous
je n'ai pas encore franchi
la ligne mince

There are blessed days
when I take a break from him
Whether or not he is there
I manage to expel him
from my protective bubble
What happiness!
My pains
give me a respite
the leech of questions
releases its pressure
the Grim Reaper
passes by
without shooting me down with a look
the infinite becomes habitable
and the house of the soul
vast enough to welcome the procession
of my helpless visitors
Master of my own time
I no longer run after harmony
I feel that I was there before her

Il y a des jours bénis
où je me repose de lui
Qu'il soit là ou non
j'arrive à l'expulser
de ma bulle de protection
Quel bonheur !
Mes douleurs
me laissent un répit
la sangsue des questions
relâche sa pression
la faucheuse
passe son chemin
sans me fusiller du regard
l'infini devient habitable
et la maison de l'âme
assez vaste pour accueillir la procession
de mes visiteurs désemparés
Maître de ma propre durée
je ne cours plus après l'harmonie
je me sens antérieur à elle

But he or she
returns
Affirming this
may I dare ask
is he, is she really
the same
What do I know about it?
I try in vain to detect the essence
of these multiple manifestations
and content myself with capturing
the subliminal and moreover
often trivial message:
Stop smoking
Do something about your OCD
Be careful not to spill on yourself
when you eat
Stop watching TV
Decide to buy
the complete works of Paganini
Don't look for a black cat
in a dark room
especially if the cat doesn't exist

Mais il ou elle
revient
En affirmant cela
je m'avance peut-être
Est-il, est-elle réellement
le, la même
Qu'en sais-je ?
De ses multiples manifestations
j'essaie en vain de déceler l'essence
et me contente d'en capter
le message subliminal
souvent trivial d'ailleurs :
Cesse de fumer
Soigne ta manie de l'ordre
Fais attention à ne pas te tacher
quand tu manges
Arrête de regarder la télévision
Décide-toi à acheter
les œuvres complètes de Paganini
Ne cherche pas le chat noir
dans la chambre noire
surtout si le chat n'existe pas

With him
I lose my sense of humor
which it seems
makes my friends glad
To lambast stupidity
his stupidity as well
and all the hellish days
is only given
to an elect few
However
and herein lies my pride
I think that my candidacy
has not been usurped
I discovered this propensity
at a late time
and deplore to see it reduced
to the suitable share
because of the shadow of a possible
fantasy that crossed my mind
So what is to be done?
as Comrade Lenin said

Avec lui
je perds mon humour
qui paraît-il
réjouit mes amis
Fustiger la bêtise
la sienne y comprise
et tous les jours que diable fait
n'est donné
qu'à une poignée d'élus
Pourtant
et c'est là que réside mon orgueil
je pense que ma candidature
n'est pas usurpée
J'ai découvert cette propension
sur le tard
et suis navré de la voir réduite
à la portion congrue
à cause d'une ombre
fantasmée si ça se trouve
Alors que faire ?
comme disait le camarade Lénine

Cultivate my uniqueness?
That's not my style
Consult?
Out of the question
Hunt down my lookalikes
ensnare them like a slave merchant
and lock them in a cargo hold?
No
I don't have that aggressiveness
Write little poems
about flowers and butterflies
or other very white and plump poems
that glorify the vanity of language?
That doesn't do much for me
when the horns of the bull
gore my hands
and the beast's breath
is burning my face
I might as well shout out to my double
while shaking the *muleta* in front of him:
Toro
come here and get it!

Cultiver mon unicité ?
Cela ne me ressemble pas
Consulter ?
Rien à faire
Me mettre en chasse de mes sosies
les attraper au filet tel un négrier
et les enfermer dans une cale ?
Non
je n'ai pas cette agressivité
Écrire des petits poèmes
sur les fleurs et les papillons
ou d'autres bien blancs et potelés
pour célébrer le nombril de la langue ?
Très peu pour moi
quand les cornes du taureau
m'écorchent les mains
et que le souffle de la bête
me brûle le visage
Autant crier à mon double
en agitant devant lui la muleta :
Toro
viens chercher !

IV

Race

Race

Race

it is because we are alone   drained   beaten down   up against the whispering Wailing Wall surrounding us above and below   With the mark of disaster   Now disparaged   Our vampiric reputation
Facing the world of Reason   Rights   and Laws
pressed down in packets of man-scars   In the obstructed deserts
On the verge of depression and suicide

and in the tuning of solitude   Our eyes grow wide   Vast organ recording the apocryphal voice canonizing the jungle and the scalp

our bodies   Jumbles of traumas   Of suppurating grafts disorganized
our radio-controlled steps   Leftovers of galaxies and mounds
We are not the haloed humans of the Book, of Art and of Spirit

we are anachronistic   We certainly are   But with regard to a certain order   Of violence
let us say that instinctively we are allergic to manuals   To sums deifying Intelligence
let us say that we do not follow those who succeed   Those who know   Those who order the magic wand and the speaking robots   Eject equations of cities   The supermen
let us say that our fear is the anguish of being   Anguish of death   Death of ourselves   With our tragic Eye
but we still have the word   The Exile of the word   The terrifying memory straddling the negative origins

we proclaim ourselves different

Race

c'est que nous sommes seuls   vidés   contrebattus   au pied du Mur-
murailles de lamentations véridiques nous encerclant dessus dessous   Avec
la marque du désastre   Maintenant décriés   Notre réputation vampiriste
Face au monde de la Raison   du Droit   et des Lois
tassés en paquets d'hommes-meurtrissures   Dans des déserts obstrués
Au bord de la dépression et du suicide

et qu'au diapason de la solitude   Nos yeux s'agrandissent   Vaste
organe enregistrant les voix apocryphes canonisant la jungle et le scalp

nos corps   Ramassis de traumatismes   De greffes suppurantes
désorganisés
notre marche téléguidée   Rebuts de galaxies et de tertres
Nous ne sommes pas les humains auréolés du Livre, de l'Art et de l'Esprit

nous sommes anachroniques   Certes nous le sommes   Mais vis-à-vis
d'un certain ordre   De violence
disons qu'instinctivement nous sommes allergiques aux manuels   Aux
sommes divinisant l'Intelligence
disons que nous ne suivons pas ceux qui réussissent   Ceux qui savent
Ceux qui ordonnent baguette magique et robots parlent   Éjectent
des cités équations   Les surhommes
disons que notre peur est angoisse d'être   Angoisse de mort
Mort de nous   Avec notre Œil tragique
mais il nous reste la parole   Exil de la parole   La mémoire
terrifiante chevauchant les genèses négatives

nous nous proclamons différents

                          first off
we barely emerge   In full debacle   Universal bankruptcy and
our wandering has only begun   For you see   It is not only
about bread and factories   Work and leisure   It is not only
about codes and borders   It is about stopping the scandal of the
anonymity of the burying of the historic oppression of an entire race
race of Atlanteans
I will explain myself
                    face to faces
                                        body to bodies
do not read
                            listen

I scream
my race rises
                        and from a condemned flesh
a ghetto of hermits
an abortion
                    my race
my purebred race
from what mass grave
             from what coitus with nothingness
                                        my race
you who dawdle in italics
                    without a prologue
                                        my race
if you pass I curse you
                    and I take your painted talismans
shove you aside in alleys
                    asphyxia
                            dead from day to day
a swearword across centuries
a curse

                        d'abord
nous émergeons à peine   En pleine débâcle   La faillite universelle et
notre errance ne fait que débuter   Car voyez-vous   Il ne s'agit pas
uniquement de pain et d'usines   De travail et de loisirs   Il ne s'agit pas
uniquement de codes et de frontières   Ils s'agit que cesse le scandale
de l'anonymat de l'enterrement de l'oppression historique de toute une race
race d'atlantes
je m'explique
            face à faces
                                corps à corps
ne lisez pas
                        écoutez

je crie
ma race monte
                    et d'une chair condamnée
un ghetto de nattaires
un avortement
                        ma race
racé ma race
de quel charnier
                de quel coït avec le néant
                                        ma race
toi qui traînes dans les italiques
                            absente de prologue
                                                ma race
si tu passes je te maudis
                    et je prends tes talismans fardés
te pousse dans les ruelles
                    asphyxie
                                morte au jour le jour
juron de par les siècles
une malédiction

                    my race
our strength nonetheless
the spring of a muscle that beats
                              the live flesh
negative fire
                    of worthlessness
the Arabs understand
a look and nightly I hit
my race which the crusades made bleed
thrown in the maw of the twentieth century
my race package of predicates
outside hunger
                    my race
the crowd and the convulsing ones
paralyzed
tapeworm in a tooth-puller's jar
                         my race
         taken in by your eyes

flaky times   Enough History   Guernica ahead   Testicles high
Damned crushed race   Bull's eye   Short farts of flame   The mule
gave us children of kings   What a beaut these precursors of earthquake
It is your turn my race   Not Aryan not cannibal but between the
contraceptives and ruminants   Butcher the hoofs of the sphinx for me
The pyramid that kills   Walk again in front of the trapdoor   Who will take
my cadavers   Sold the mousetrap   You know the tune   You and me
we will see the absolution of the bulls   But the language yes the language
I learn to reason at the threshold of letters   Ali and Fatima will no longer
read Bachir and his friends   Thus the chechia   The street kids who
nonetheless win prizes   Gifted despite all   The old legend of assimilation
We are hung over a normal thing with drinking the dregs   "Civilizations I hate
you"   Me I tell you I water down your narcotics   No drugs for forgetting
No neon nearness   But ritualized fighting of the recent Rif war   By this I
mean to say   Explosive mixture   And give you an earful

                    ma race
notre force cependant
le ressort d'un muscle qui bat
                              la chair vive
feu négatif
                des nèfles
les Arabes comprennent
un regard et nuitamment je frappe
ma race qui fut sang de croisades
jetée dans la gueule du vingtième siècle
ma race paquet de prédicats
dehors la faim
                    ma race
la foule et les convulsionnaires
paralysie
ténia dans un bocal d'arracheur de dents
                          ma race
        et prends sur tes yeux

temps floche   Histoire Basta   Guernica devant   Testicules haut
Patatras fichtre race   Le doigt dans l'œil   À ras pet d'incendie   La mule
nous a donné des enfants de rois   Ils sont beaux les précurseurs de séisme
Et race à ton tour   Pas aryenne pas cannibale mais entre le
contraceptifs et les ruminants   Charcute-moi ces sabots de sphinx
La pyramide qui tue   Encore marche devant la trappe   Qui voudra
de mes cadavres   Adjugée la souricière   On connaît la musique   Nous
verrons tous vous et moi l'absolution des taureaux   Mais le langage oui le
langage   J'apprends à raisonner au seuil des lettres   Ali et Fatima ne liront
plus Bachir et ses amis   La chéchia donc   Les yaouled qui
décrochent les prix   Doués malgré tout   La vieille légende de l'assimilation
Nous cuvons les dépôts chose normale des piquettes   « Civilisations je
vous hais »   Moi je dis je vous abreuve stupéfiants   Pas drogues pour
oublier   Pas promiscuité de néon   Mais baroud de la pas trop vieille guerre
du Rif   Je m'entends   Mélange détonant   Et prends sur tes oreilles

The sun will no longer rise in the east   Your blue zeal
Agadir the sardines human sardines walled up in tin become
thistle-men-thistle free to putrify wherever it pleases them
But no there is the Koutoubia the tombs of the Marinids the tombs of
the Saadians and the legend of Chellah.
Budget of ruins
race to dig in again to the height of the glands
further on
    race
        named within my blackouts

distinguished
        my race
what an orgy of the maimed
you remember the Andalusian inebriations
the baptismal fonts
        the doglike arabesque
you remember
        Granada
                the bitch
1492
    the Genoese caravels
you remember
        Charles Martel
an impossible uchronia
    my race
and the crowd
    the horde
that of Ramadan or celebration
the ablutions at the Moorish bath
the armpit and the groin shorn
the spasms of the gates
        a madwoman

Le soleil ne se lèvera plus à l'est   Ton zèle bleu   Agadir les sardines hommes-sardines   murés   fer-blanc   devenus   chardon-hommes-chardons libres de croupir où ça leur plaît   Mais non il y a la Koutoubia les tombeaux des Mérinides les tombeaux des Saâdiens et la légende du Chellah
Budget de ruines
race à creuser encore à la hauteur des glandes
plus loin
    race
        nommée dans mes syncopes

racé
        ma race
quelle orgie de mutilés
tu te rappelles les cuites andalouses
les vasques
        l'arabesque de chien
tu te rappelles
        Grenade
            la garce
1492
    les caravelles du Génois
tu te rappelles
        Charles Martel
une uchronie impossible
    ma race
et la foule
    la horde
celle de ramadan ou fête
les ablutions au bain maure
l'aisselle et l'aine qu'on tond
les spasmes de portails
        une folle

                        my race
ruffle your veils
the horns lie at the bottom of the well
a bullet
          your sidewalks and your alleyways
                      your gutted trash cans
the crowd
          your public fountains
                      your feeding troughs
broken
          embargo
                forbidden zone
                            my race
Arab quarter
                tent city
                  shantytown
there you lie my race
                you scream through your latrines
                        your torture pits
fourth-class carriage
                with livestock
                        my race
sold at auction
          between two corridors
                who can bid higher
                                my race
and shut up   shut up   shut up
                          my race
drop dead
          swallow your scorched earth
the eye sinks
stigmata and statelessness
I thrash you my race
I scream at you from the East and from the West
neither this

                    ma race
hérisse tes voiles
au fond du puits gisent les cornes
une balle
            tes pavés et tes ruelles
                        tes poubelles éventrées
la foule
            tes fontaines publiques
                        tes mangeoires
fauchée
        embargo
                zone interdite
                                ma race
médina
                douar
                    bidonville
tu gis ma race
                tu cries tes latrines
                            tes fosses de torture
wagon de quatrième classe
                    avec le bétail
                            ma race
vendue aux enchères
            entre deux couloirs
                        qui dit mieux
                                    ma race
et tais-toi   tais-toi   tais-toi
                                ma race
claque
        gobe ton brûlis
l'œil chavire
des stigmates et apatride
je te cogne ma race
te gueule à l'Orient et à l'Occident
ni ceci

             nor that
but you
             the ultimate race

who murders me in my race
                              each millennium
and sprouts up
                   bundles of graft
                                    on my way
who then stirs my roots
I remember
there was no water in the beginning
but a rolling stretch of sand like a floating caravan of continents
a shifting of dunes
there was only the tom-tom of mutations
a carnivorous lifting
and me crocodile bard
                              delighting myself with lava
there was only the sulfurous presence of fire
the putrid garlic of high pressure
the fetid saurian crests

who murders me in the whisper
of everyday being
                   in my hibernation
I remember
the night had turned
                              extinct in the spiral of flames
an elastic clay piled on my forehead
nomadic monkeys snickered

     ni cela
mais toi
    l'ultime race

qui m'assassine dans ma race
          chaque millénaire
et pousse
      fagots de greffes
           sur mon passage
qui donc remue mes racines
je me remémore
il n'y avait pas d'eau à l'origine
mais un roulis d'ergs comme une caravane flottante de continents
un tangage de dunes
il n'y avait que le tam-tam des mutations
une levée de carnassiers
et moi barde-crocodile
         me délectant de lave
il n'y avait que la présence sulfureuse du feu
l'ail putride des hautes tensions
les crêtes fétides de sauriens

qui m'assassine dans mon murmure d'être
chaque jour
      dans mon hibernation
je me remémore
la nuit avait obliqué
          éteinte dans la spirale des flammes
une glaise élastique s'entassait sur mon front
des singes transhumants ricanaient

was I a totem
      a Saharan monolith
or this bodily clarity of lightning

who
who then amputated germs from me
in this porous ablation
      of the night

then I plot it
black
   alone
      with salvos of ink
the uncountable conspiracy of destitute races
the seventh decade of the last sun
will see me monarch
deliver thus mother
      earth of beggar kings
spatter this fluid on me
     this venom of power
let me be born
     like a carbuncle
on the third eye of my accomplices

I fall
  to the lowest floors of clichéd minarets
cling
  spider frozen to the steps of the clouds
bolt your flanks
     mother
trundle of drunken ditches
jealous of my rising

étais-je totem
                        menhir saharien
ou cette corporelle éclaircie de la foudre

qui
qui donc m'a amputé de germes
dans cette ablation poreuse
                        de la nuit

alors je l'ourdis
noir
          seul
                    à salves d'encre
l'innombrable complot des races déchues
la septième décade du dernier soleil
me verra monarque
accouche donc mère
                      terre de rois-mendiants
gicle-moi ce fluide
                  ce venin de pouvoir
fais-moi naître
                  comme furoncle
sur le troisième œil de mes complices

je chute
      aux bas étages des minarets-poncifs
m'accroche
      araignée glacée aux marches des nuages
verrouille tes flancs
                  mère
gigogne de fossés ivres
jalouse de ma levée

you stuff with salt
        the itinerary of my wounds

I plot it
        weave it even more beautifully
this conspiracy of aphasic tribes
since the scandal of my birth
since the plunder of my conception
I made sure of your members
despot with a thunderbolt belly

primary weapon
        my head parries
                fends off the shields
and I plot it
        in the cranial pits
                the golden ruins
this conspiracy of faded races
stale seeds
        delivered to the sands
so my cosmogonic blood
        can be reborn

what
        my race
rage
I have proclaimed your pervert eyes
I have retraced your reversed cycles
the injurious dawn
        and your worn-out hieroglyphs

tu farcis de sel
                l'itinéraire de mes blessures

je l'ourdis
                le tisse de plus belle
ce complot des tribus aphasiques
depuis le scandale de ma naissance
depuis le brigandage de ma conception
je me suis assuré de tes membres
despote au ventre foudroyant

arme première
                ma tête pare
                              charge les boucliers
et je l'ourdis
                sur les crâniennes
                              les ruines d'or
ce complot des race éteintes
graines éventées
                livrées aux sables
afin que renaisse
                mon sang cosmogonique

quoi
                ma race
fureur
j'ai clamé tes yeux pervers
j'ai retracé tes cycles à rebours
l'aube délétère
                et tes hiéroglyphes à l'usure

we will say wisdom
                all that geometric expectation
the adventure of the spirit

they have said all recounted all demonstrated all
and you
       still night
            tumult of guardians
by my lot
undefeated offspring
here you are rebellious
                exhibiting your wombs
the insufficiency of exile
no more words no more words
                      will you speak
the ark of the drums
                you come out
torn asphalt
            flags and banners
dictated cadence
                never so uprooted

and with your exile of mandrake
                  I remake my perception
a probe in my brain
may your drums carry me
                son of Haddaoua
my father spat in my mouth
                      the saliva of immunity
black fire
          the thread of hemp
                the bacteria arcade
frenzied pact

on dira sagesse
    toute cette attente géométrique
l'aventure de l'esprit

ils ont tout dit tout raconté tout démontrée
et toi
  encore nuit
    tumulte de veilleurs
par mes partages
progéniture insoumise
te voilà rebelle
    exhibant tes matrices
l'insuffisance de l'exil
plus de mots plus de mots
      parleras-tu
l'arche des tambours
    tu sors
asphalte déchiré
    drapeaux et banderoles
la cadence dictée
    jamais autant déracinée

et dans ton exil de mandragore
     je refais ma perception
un stylet dans mon cerveau
que vos tambours m'emportent
    fils de Haddaoua
mon père m'a craché dans la bouche
      la salive d'immunité
feu noir
  le fil de chanvre
    l'arcade bactérie
pacte frénésie

                    talus tambour
green virgins red virgins
black fire
            embers in my throat
the pact that binds my head that I offer the balm that offers me
I stay I depart
drool
      guardians of my body
the eye detaches itself
                I kiss your feet
march march venerable scorpions
                             I kiss your stings
and you master of all pythons
                         peace be upon you

tambour
            tambourine
                    I check my body
my head ratchet
            kick kick
                son of Aîssaoua
aim
        my capsizing heaven
Gods Devils
treasures and jars will no longer escape me
tambour tambourine
            crotales
I pursue your hoop
                    the alley commands me
I bark
may I be married to Aïcha Oandicha in the castles of sorcery
She has hooves they say

tambour tambourine

                tambour talus
vierges vertes vierges rouges
feu noir
        braises dans mon gosier
le pacte qui me lie la tête que j'offre le baume qui m'offre
je reste je pars
bavez
    gardes de mon corps
l'œil se détache
          j'embrasse vos pieds
marchez marchez vénérables scorpions
                  je baise vos dards
et toi maître de tous les pythons
                  paix sur toi

tambour
            tambourin
                je vérifie mon corps
ma tête crécelle
            ruez ruez
                fils de Aïssaoua
épaulez
            mon ciel chavire
Dieux Diables
les trésors et les jarres ne m'échapperont plus
tambour tambourin
            crotales
je poursuis ton cerceau
                le ruelle me dicte
j'aboie
que l'on me marie avec Aïcha Qandicha dans les châteaux de sorcellerie
Elle a des sabots qu'on dit

tambour tambourin

                        I burn incense to the point of suffocation
boiling water for my ablutions
then Melegueta pepper and the most beautiful cantharidins
go out and cut clubs of sandalwood
don't interrupt me
I go back into my sleep
the spirits galvanize me
it is time to say
                      why I am vomiting the world

elsewhere
from that demented crowd beyond the seven seas
elsewhere
curved matrix beyond my trances
crowd
sun lubricating my words
elsewhere
articulated beyond a meteoric gesture that strangles the circle
into a public of crazy bleeding
people
the Atlantean history of galaxies in rut
here I am going back to the roots
of the ax where I bleed
elsewhere
spatters of naphtha on the writing
body
like a localized earthquake
hands of diviners from which flamethrowers grow

                        j'encens jusqu'à la suffocation
de l'eau bouillante pour mes ablutions
des maniguettes alors et les plus belles cantharides
sortez et coupez des gourdins de santal
ne m'interrompez pas
je rentre dans mon sommeil
des esprits me galvanisent
il est temps de dire
                        pourquoi je dégueule le monde

ailleurs
de cette foule démente au-delà des sept mers
ailleurs
matrice incurvée au-delà de mes transes
foule
soleil lubrifiant ma parole
ailleurs
articulée au-delà d'un geste météorite qui strangule le cercle
en publics de peuples fous
saignants
l'histoire atlante de galaxies en rut
v'là que je remonte les racines
de la cognée où je saigne
ailleurs
giclée de naphte sur l'écrit
corps
comme un séisme localisé
mains de sourciers auxquelles poussent des lance-flammes

elsewhere
no life is possible
except kidnapping
beyond a night when one kills each other
                                        under the bad star

elsewhere
the pitching bow
                of carcasses of races
headlands that extinguish signs
crypts of padlocked dreams
universal cardiac silences
elsewhere the eye of hilarious gods
dinosaurian guard of cryptograms
our surging history
                at the epicenter of the magma

elsewhere
                the same gods
in crazy circles
the strike of the gods smashing the sarcophagi the armor of gold of bronze
volcanic fracas ejecting in monstrous scoria
the crazy gods
mad about the fourteenth century
                              and about the abduction
particularly the uprising of the gods
in the arteries of human concentrations

elsewhere
very much elsewhere
a billion robot-men
exorcising after the earth

ailleurs
nulle vie n'est possible
hormis le rapt
au-delà d'une nuit où s'entretuer
                                     à la mauvaise étoile

ailleurs
tangue de proues
                de carcasses de races
de promontoires extincteurs de signes
de cryptes cadenas de rêves
de silences cardiaques universels
ailleurs l'œil de dieux hilares
garde dinosaurienne de cryptogrammes
notre histoire sourdre
                à l'épicentre du magma

ailleurs
                mêmes dieux
en cercles fous
la grève des dieux défonçant les sarcophages les armures d'or de bronze
fracas de volcan éjectant en scories monstres
les dieux fous
fous du siècle quatorze
                        et du rapt
nommément le soulèvement des dieux
dans les artères des concentrations humaines

ailleurs
bien ailleurs
un milliard d'hommes-robots
exorcisant après la terre

```
                        the sky
and elsewhere
                two billion ostrich-men
earth belly flat out belly to earth
one sky above the other
the chill
it is not about fatalisms
```

```
and the overlooking earth
I tell you
man will speak
                        his reign will arrive
frizzy mane
                cyclopean
Totem    Totem    Totem
                            new paganism
in short stampede of fragments
                        the cataract is arming itself
except the apocalyptic night that will see brain on brain grow heavy weighing
cadaver on cadaver to salt head on head tower of rebels and pariahs tower of
men
it turns
            your bitch of an earth
                            and you with it
whoa
    I speak to the archi-plural of the fault
races from now on mass fucking everywhere
brachycephalic here
                        dolichocephalic there
white palms
                glass eyes
on stilts or pygmy
```

                              le ciel
et ailleurs
                  deux milliards d'hommes-autruches
terre-ventre ventre-terre
un ciel au-dessus de l'autre
la crève
il ne s'agit pas de fatalismes

et terre surplombe
je vous le dis
l'homme parlera
                      son règne arrivera
crinière crépue
            cyclopéenne
Totem   Totem   Totem
                            nouveau paganisme
à ras galopade de débris
                      s'arme la cataracte
sauf nuit d'apocalypse verra s'alourdir cerveau sur cerveau plomber cadavre
sur cadavre saler tête sur tête tour de rebelles et de parias tour
d'hommes
elle tourne
            votre putain de terre
                            et vous avec
holà
    je parle à l'archi-pluriel de la faute
races désormais coïtant en pagaille
qui brachycéphale
                      qui dolichocéphale
paumes blanches
            œils de verre
échasses ou pygmées

in the heap of dialogues
the m i x

I
   cancerous
a banished break rocking
                            rocking
seismography of myth
                            rocking rocking
to the archi-plural of fault
nudity
I saw you all
               belly to belly
in single file
                        in front of the monster
he laughed the most ugliest   a clay paw on your necks   The other in
the confines of your souls   The monster fucked sadistically   Watching
the shooting stars   Jets   artificial satellites   the astronauts
in sporting outfits outside their ships   And your eyes did not
break away from his dripping magnetism

catastrophe   catastrophe
near my voice
                the old world
                       old monster
between you and me
                old scores to settle
catastrophe   catastrophe
near by
                exploding cancer
old world
                      old leprosy
                                slipping

sur le tas des dialogues
le m é l a n g e

je
   cancéreux
tangue bannie brisure
                            tangue
sismographie du mythe
                       tangue tangue
à l'archi-pluriel de la faute
nudité
je vous ai vus
               nombril au nombril
à la queue leu leu
                     devant le monstre
il riait de plus laide   une patte d'argile sur vos nuques   L'autre aux
confins de vos âmes   Le monstre baisait avec sadisme   En regardant
passer les étoiles filantes   les Jets   les satellites artificiels   les astronautes
en tenue de sport en dehors de leurs vaisseaux   Et vos yeux ne se détachaient
pas de son magnétisme dégoulinant

la catastrophe   la catastrophe
à deux pas de ma voix
                    vieux monde
                              vieux monstre
entre toi et moi
                  de vieux comptes à régler
la catastrophe   la catastrophe
à deux pas
                    cancer détonant
vieux monde
                        vieux lèpre
                                    dérapant

without fossil without idiom the squaring
                                       the seven heads of the myth
without compass without axis
                 locust history
old world old leprosy
                         hurtling down
it is the moment it is the word
that raises me up from the quadrupeds
                 the whole body
                               congenital strength
to the archi-plural of the fault
namely
             stop
                 turn around
the monster greets you well

in advance
     indelible trap
in advance
     skirmish beyond memory
in advance
     hand
that writes it here the dry drained of its tortures
the root that springs out again from the mass grave
fascinated meteorite
               the indecent eye
hand
     our night among you

in advance
         the rush that devours us
d e a t h   teaching me
                   epic of risk

sans fossile sans idiome la quadrature
                                                les sept têtes du mythe
sans boussole sans axe
                histoire acridienne
vieux monde vieille lèpre
                      dévalant
c'est le moment c'est le mot
me dresse de quadrupèdes
                  corps entier
                                      force congénitale
à l'archi-pluriel de la faute
nommément
                halte
                    demi-tour
le monstre vous salue bien

d'avance
      traquenard indélébile
d'avance
      échauffourée hors mémoire
d'avance
       main
qui l'écrit l'aride vidé de ses supplices
qui la racine resurgie du charnier
qui météorite fascinée
                l'œil risqué
main
      notre nuit parmi vous

d'avance
         la ruée qui nous dévore
m o r t   m'apprenant
                        épopée du risque

done like the miraculous cadaver
I said
                        my incompatibility with you
I said
                        the orgasm of crime
and my incompatibility
                with you
I have in front of me my body and the framework of nothingness
I lie on that pyramid of nothingness between the talons of civilization
of writing
            of steel
of lead between the eyes
I am laid out
    beardless Paleolithic
you knew it Fanon
back to back
              everyone for himself
that was too brief
                the war
                          matter of extinction
they wore us down
our star is dying
                  before before coming to term

catastrophe   catastrophe
in your shacks
              in your palaces
a little bit more well-off
                      a little more hungry
"civilized"
              carnivorous at any level
I saw you
            belly to belly
face down
              in front of the monster

quitte comme le cadavre miraculeux
j'ai dit
                      mon incompatibilité de vous
j'ai dit
                      l'orgasme du crime
et mon incompatibilité
                  de vous
j'ai devant moi mon corps et l'armature du néant
je gis sur cette pyramide du néant entre les serres de la civilisation
de l'écrit
              de l'acier
du plomb entre les yeux
je gis
    paléolithique imberbe
tu le savais Fanon
dos à dos
            chacun pour soi
ce fut trop bref
                la guerre
                            matière d'extinction
on nous a eus à l'usure
notre étoile se meurt
                avant-avant terme

la catastrophe   la catastrophe
dans vos cases
                dans vos palais
un peu plus nantis
                    un peu plus affamés
« civilisés »
                carnivores à n'importe quelle échelle
je vous ai vus
              nombril au nombril
à plat ventre
              devant le monstre

he was bursting out laughing imitating Zeus   Threw narcotic seeds at you one by one   He would get a multi-sex hard on and would languorously rape you while your offspring reaped his sperm for the mindlessly stupefying fecundity of your females   And your bodies would shrivel up   Dwindle   Contract into varicose veins in fragments of schist

Nudity
        my stature
the terrifying scalpel of migrations
I am of this flint
memory returns to me
poetry
        the word given
                from man to man

some celestial bodies rise
        to render a last tribute
it is not my voice that will make the steel of conquest stop
it is not my hand
        to barely strangle
                grindstone of lingering ones
word   c r y
        this seismic cry alone
hurtling down
        the other one public
the thirst to only be the mark of the pariah
the thirst to bog down fate the other one
the thirst of all   r e v o l u t i o n
planet
        remnants of spattered blood
o naïve ones

il s'esclaffait imitant Zeus   Vous jetait graine par graine ses pavots somnifères   Il bandait multi-sexes et vous violait langoureusement pendant que votre progéniture récoltait son sperme pour la fécondité abêtissante de vos femelles   Et vos corps se rétrécissaient S'amenuisaient   Se contractaient en varices en éclats de schiste

Nudité
   ma stature
le terrifiant scalpel des migrations
je suis de ce silex
me revient la mémoire
poésie
    parole donnée
       d'hommes à hommes

des astres montent
     dernier tribut à rendre
ce n'est pas ma voix qui fera s'arrêter l'acier des conquêtes
ce n'est pas ma main
    juguler à peine
         meule d'attardés
parole c r i
     ce cri de séisme seul
à dévaler
    public l'autre
la soif de n'être que la marque du paria
la soif d'enliser destin l'autre
la soif de toute r é v o l u t i o n
planète
    restant de sangs éparpillés
ô naïfs

          from top to bottom
putting up with the litanies of mourners
in cannonade whips
brother you are calling me
and I have nothing to do with your fraternity of scapegoats   Of historic spectators   Bygone people   I name you publics 100 publics and more of the fourteenth century   Cleaners   Sufferers   Publics not people on benches   on benches
my brotherhood moves itself rhythmically unloading from all borders
Uprooting evil from the inaudible body   Arid venomous stride of the tit
Free free   The passkey for which I take responsibility   It's a race that refuses triumphant idolatry   The right above the belt   Race profoundly mine   In no way do I find it captured in the public stopped in front of the windows and lofts of the street entertainers   Tossed in the dumpsters. But in my body   Its rolling   By millennial osmosis
A t a v i s m s

Atlantis
                    may I demythologize you
                                  your eruptive resurge
from the very depths of the pagan condemnation
you are fused as a talking race
                        as a displacing race
you will not tattoo archipelagoes with swastikas
                                you will not kill
the voices of the dead
          the earth indents in violence
I see I see the anarchy of creation
one god was making laws
                  the other sabotaging
The Humid is Dry
of this duality the deadly confection
to die in the height of enjoyment
it matters little to me to know if other planets are populated

           de haut en bas
encaissant les litanies de pleureuses
en cravaches canonnades
frère m'appelez-vous
et je n'ai que faire de votre fraternité de boucs émissaires   De spectateurs
historiques   Peuples révolus   Je vous nomme publics   100 publics et plus
du siècle quatorze   Ravaleurs   Subisseurs   Publics non plus peuples
sur des bancs   sur des bancs
ma fraternité se meut décharge scandante de toutes frontières   Déracinant
le mal du corps inaudible Foulée aguerrie de venin de la mamelle
Libre libre   Le passe-partout que je reprends à mon compte   C'est une race
qui refuse l'idolâtrie triomphant   Le droit de dessus la ceinture   Race
profondément mienne   Je ne la retrouve nullement dans les publics arrêtés
aux vitrines et greniers des saltimbanques   Culbutés dans les
dépotoirs   Mais dans mon corps   Son roulis   Par osmose millénaire
A t a v i s m e s

Atlantide
                    que je te démythologise
                                  te résurge éruptif
du fin fond de la condamnation païenne
te remerge en race parlante
                          en race déplaceuse
tu ne tatoueras la archipels de svastikas
                                  tu ne tueras point
voix des morts
              la terre s'échancre à la violence
je vois je vois l'anarchie de la création
un dieu légiférait
                       l'autre sabotait
Sec l'Humide
de cette dualité la confection mortelle
crever au summum de la jouissance
il m'importe peu de savoir si d'autres astres sont peuplés

It took me a long time to come to know the force of the gods of the moment
The strategy of their victory   I had to drink from the source of their abuses
the excretions of potentates
Atlantis first milestone
Indecent Writing Words
              will follow you
and in the new organized chaos
                      nothing more will germinate

and jungler
at the height of pleasure
nobody has ever crashed into my body
I may hang myself
I may curse you as I have already cursed your ancestors
eat brothers and procreate
the monster lavishes you with blessings

       west
          at
point-blank
    range
mouth of filth and shoot into the crowd
there will be men left over
and shoot again on the topography of iron curtains
I lost the North and South
the dehumanized East-West
anachronism

Il a fallu de mémoire longue que je sache la force des dieux du moment
La stratégie de leur victoire   Il m'a fallu boire à la source de leurs
sévices l'excrétion des potentats
Atlantide premier jalon
Écrit Parole risqués
                te suivront
et sur le nouveau chaos organisé
                    rien plus ne germera

or jungler
au summum de la jouissance
personne n'a jamais télescopé mon corps
il m'arrivera de me pendre
il m'arrivera de vous maudire comme j'ai déjà maudit vos ancêtres
mangez mes frères et procréez
le monstre vous prodigue sa bénédiction

occident
    à
  bout
 portant
gueule d'immondices et tire dans le tas
il restera des hommes
et re-tire sur la topographie des rideaux de fer
j'ai perdu le Nord et le Sud
l'anachronisme Est-Ouest
déshumain

                    not of the social race
scalped three times
                    asphalted over for rebellion of hemorrhaging
a thundering body
West
                    splinter-brand of the recalled pariah
bullet target   putrid javelin
                        that I receive from our cowardice
old whore
            morbid pasture
and the bitch oriental nigger girl
                    to ravish you
                                sabbath customers
(I cured myself of her magnetisms as of our fatalisms)
West
            the last caesarian
                        the last word
before before   my inexpressible
                            s h e d d i n g

mine   mine
                    the crucible moons
melting
        eardrums
            electrified idioms
the green mountain rises and spins
ride   ride the tide with no future arc
my ancestors of the highest branch rise
geometry of the terrifying ones
be gone my reason
                        the desert and the anvil
the oligarchy of temples restituted by lightning
the land registries of all civilization

                        pas de la race sociale
scalpé trois fois
                        bitumé pour rébellion d'hémorragie
un corps tonitruant
Occident
                        tison-écharde du paria remémoré
balle-cible   javelot putride
                        que je reçois de nos lâchetés
vieille putain
                morbide pâture
et la garce orientale-nègre
                        te ravir
                                clientèle de sabbat
(je me suis guéri de ses magnétismes comme de nos fatalismes)
Occident
                la dernière césarienne
                        le dernier mot
avant avant   mon inénarrable
                                        m u e

à moi   à moi
                les lunes du creuset
fonte
      tympans
            idiomes électrifiés
monte la montagne verte et tourbillonne
monte   monte la marée sans arche de futur
montent mes ancêtres de plus haute branche
géométrie des terrifiants
va ma raison
            le désert et l'enclume
l'oligarchie des temples restitués par la foudre
les cadastres de toute civilisation

    go
        my equator hand
anchor of equinoxes
go live as a nomad in the salt flats
                toward more illustrious pharaohs
more colossal pyramids
smash clear the enigmatic dregs
make inertia explode
        your enduring

at
point-blank
range
sing sing Oum Kalthoum
for the delirium of the Arabic people
dilate with a vice this sexual protuberance
the black gold will wean the Impeccable ones
pride of the bastard in jubilation
pride of the world attacking our power
pride of the fiefdom
rigid pride passing by our heads
our mugs of final prophets
our skeletons too many
        for the world
they will accuse us of intolerance
pride the promised and postponed ride
serenity of pride

point blank and profane the Unraped aped One   Sing Oum Kalthoum in full cybernetic   Sing the Nile   The spectacular dams   Your pyramids and ours   The hearts of descending centuries   Crazy love   Suspended

    va
           ma main équateur
                    ancre d'équinoxes
nomadise dans les salines
                vers de plus illustres pharaons
de plus colossales pyramides
fracasse net les vases énigmatiques
explose l'inertie
        ta durée

à
bout
portant
chante chante Oum Kalthoum
pour le délire des peuples arabes
dilate ce sexe protubérance à l'étau
l'or noir sevra les Impeccables
orgueil du bâtard en liesse
orgueil le monde attente à notre puissance
orgueil du fief
orgueil rigide passant par nos têtes
nos gueules d'ultimes prophètes
nos squelettes en trop
                pour le monde
on nous accusera d'intolérance
orgueil la chevauchée promise et reculée
sérénité de l'orgueil

à bout portant et profane l'Inviolé   Chante Oum Kalthoum en pleine cybernétique Chante le Nil   Les barrages spectaculaires   Tes pyramides et les nôtres   Les cœurs de siècles descendants L'amour fou   Suspendues

quaternary periods   Do not fear to accumulate clichés   My gazelle in Niagaras of perfume   Forgetfulness sowing its rosary of romances   The traces of the campsite and the mount   The mounting eye   Burst in glassy tarantula stares   Abysses slashed in honeyed faucets   In pipes of sacramental milk
Sing a little if not for the funeral it will be for the procession   Sing that I may write the Book of the Dead   The oral testament of submissive races   May I make less vapid the malediction that has struck us at the top of the graft   May I order an exemplary retreat of Creation   May I show insolence to the bushy misery of internal jungles   Sing your voice moves us and makes us laugh at the height of enjoyment

"the multitudes stopped to attest to how in my uniqueness I edify
the foundations of glory"

Sing the arid Crescent   Sing the wailing wall me I skirt the wall of shame   Sing the exhumed broken down Star of the Orient Sing a little that I give you my eyes   Your fetish love for the agile toe of Africa violated in cyclic ceremonies   Sing the impossibility of the arm arresting the tool   The impossibility of the hand arresting the body The impossible pride of your undone race

Nightingale cry of imbecilic poets   Cry of flashing rage of weeded meteors   Cry of the gut at the edge of abattoirs   Cry of the secular waste intimating the Arrest
cry of the bulimic concentrations of money
cry of the miraculous treasures hanging from sorcerers
cry of the learned quackery resulting from following power
cry hailed from the flanks of genocide
cry medieval light of obscure epochs
cry I skid on the rails of chaos

quarternaires   Ne crains pas d'accumuler les clichés   Ma gazelle aux niagaras de parfums   L'oubli semant son chapelet de romances   Les traces du campement et la monture   L'œil monte Eclate en regards de tarentules vitreuses   Abîmes tailladés en robinets de miel   En tuyaux de lait sacramental   Chante un peu si ce n'est pour l'ordre funèbre ce sera pour le cortège   Chante que j'écrive le Livre des morts   Le testament oral des races soumises   Que je désemmièvre la malédiction qui nous a frappés au sommet de la greffe   Que j'ordonne à la Création une déroute exemplaire   Que j'insolence la misère touffue des jungles intérieures   Chante ta voix nous pourfend et nous fait rire au summum de la jouissance

« les peuples se sont arrêtés pour attester comment dans mon unicité j'édifie les bases de la gloire »

Chante le Croissant aride   Chante le mur des lamentations moi je côtoie le mur de la honte   Chante étoile déterreuse d'Orient tombé en panne Chante un peu que je te donne mes yeux   Ton amour fétiche à l'orteil agile de l'Afrique violée en cérémonies cycliques   Chante l'impossible du bras appréhendant l'outil   L'impossible de la main appréhendant le corps L'impossible orgueil de ta race défaite

Cri du rossignol des poètes imbéciles   Cri de la rage clignotante d'aérolithes sarclés Cri de la tripe à l'orée des abattoirs   Cri du gâchis séculaire intimant l'Arrêt
cri des concentrations boulimie de l'argent
cri des trésors miraculés suspendus aux sorciers
cri charlatanerie docte à la suite du pouvoir
cri salué des flancs du génocide
cri médiéval lumière des époques obscures
cri je patine sur les rails du chaos

cry the changed wind will stop locusts gesticulating
cry packed to the edge of memory that has become organ
cry of the Continent the tam-tam covers us with voices
cry throat you contain only my most ridiculous detonations
cry I am more than a man something someone in tragic expansion
cry incandescent casting of mine
cry I will drown this planet in an asphyxiating poetry
raw jackhammer gas that I reserve
cry I know how to speak but not to the powerful
cry   o b j e c t o r
cry the treason of the friend   of deportation speech
cry the howling tour of stagnation
cry the belched bile in hoisted quadrilaterals
cry prostitution of the musician monkey to the point of twisting
cry the critico-philosophical insolence
burying us alive in our name
cry that we leave alone the bastards that we are
cry Enough

shameless songstress   Old hetaera   Scalping us in febrile blood Hoodwinking us   Dropping us insignificant and strawlike into the brotherhood of sensory delirium   Out of a lyricism mutations of all faculties that we fart   Happily tapping us on our mutual thighs and backs
      Purring the imbecilic refrain of the brotherhood of exclusion Sing Oum Kalthoum your voice slays us and makes us laugh at the height of pleasure

carnivorous fossil   Sister of the surprised mammoth   But incalculable f o r c e

cri le vent s'arrêtera changé criquets à la gesticulation
cri tassé à la lie de la mémoire devenue organe
cri de Continent le tam-tam nous couvre des voix
cri gosier tu ne contiens que la plus dérisoire de mes détonations
cri je suis plus qu'homme quelque chose quelqu'un en tragique expansion
cri coulée mienne incandescente
cri je noierai cette planète d'une poésie asphyxiante
marteau-piqueur gaz bruts que je réserve
cri je sais parler mais pas aux puissants
cri   o b j e c t e u r
cri la trahison de l'ami   du déporte-parole
cri les dégueulades tournées du marasme
cri la bile renvoyée en quadrilatères hissés
cri prostitution du musicien singe à se tordre
cri la morgue philosophale criticaillante
nous enterrant en notre nom vivants
cri qu'on foute la paix aux salauds que nous sommes
cri Assez

impudique chanteuse   Vieille hétaïre   Nous scalpant dans le sang fébrile
Nous embobinant   Nous lâchant fétu et paille à la fraternité du délire
sensitif   D'un lyrisme que nous pétons mutations de toutes facultés
Nous tapant sur les cuisses et les dos mutuels   Ronronnant
l'imbécile refrain de la fraternité d'exclusion   Chante Oum Kalthoum
ta voix nous pourfend et nous fait rire au summum de la jouissance

fossile carnivore   Sœur du mammouth surpris   Mais incalculable
f o r c e

Maghreb! Maghreb!
segregated fingers of the buried hand
transvestite stature of the sphinx
Maghreb with pierced hands

the deadline for the great shedding has arrived   Deboning of the collective   Softening of the brain   Transfusion bloods ochre   The control of organs   Prognostic of old rotten foundations   Break citadel of thinking men   Old and fresh new accounts to pay for   To disclose unmask cleanse   Break and fall apart   Diarrhea blasts from the anus of the world   Point-blank at audiences and tyrants   Swaggering senility   The circus of deaf-mutes   The tribunal of the lame   Gangs with kilometric Havana cigar-ransom-checks   Gangs for hire   Gangs drumming in political poster leaflet and reflected in your corner   Historic gangs   Trophies for museums oh gangs inseminating the ruse ancestrally strained for the congelation of the species   Gangs of a science swinging down its cleavers   Claws more inhuman than the barbaric cry   Old world ruminating   Spraying with mortal juices our mouths of prophets in the trap of the hungry whale   Old world and our so-called youth in dense hemorrhage

Enough
    I   l i v e
here I am in all my boilers
all glands erect
my orifices pressed for time
I descend to my hells
        my underworld of moths
dictate and re-dictate
thus I rediscover myself
        in the farthest depths of the embryo
equal to my stature

Maghreb ! Maghreb !
doigts ségrégés de la main enfouie
stature de sphinx travesti
Maghreb aux mains trouées

elle est parvenue l'échéance de la grande mue   Décarcassement collectif
Décalcarisation cervelles   Transfusion sangs ocre   Le contrôle des organes
Prognostic des vielles bases pourries   Craque citadelle d'hommes pensants
Comptes vieux et frais à régler   Dévoiler démasquer démaquiller   Craque
et flanche   La diarrhée pète à l'anus du monde   À bout portant publics
et tyrans   Sénilité bravades   Le chapiteau des sourds-muets   Le
tribunal des éclopés   Gangs à cigares-havane-chèques-rançons
kilométriques   Gangs à gages   Gangs l'affiche le tract coup de massue
et réfléchis dans ton coin   Gangs historiques   Trophées pour les
musées ô gangs inséminant la ruse ancestralement tendue pour la congélation
de l'espèce   Gangs d'une science dévalant ses hachoirs   Serres plus
inhumaines que le cri barbare   Vieux monde ruminant   Arrosant de sucs
mortels nos gueules de prophètes à la trappe de la baleine famélique   Vieux
monde et notre prétendue jeunesse en hémorragie dense

Assez
       je   v i s
me voici dans toutes mes chaudières
érectant de toutes glandes
mes orifices pressés
je descends à mes enfers
            mes souterrains de phalènes
dicte et redicte
ainsi je me redécouvre
            au tréfonds de l'embryon
égal à ma stature

                        egg of infinities
millions of possibilities
                                gestation of peoples
                                            of continents
humanity wiggling
                        and voice
c h a n g i n g
                I escape
                I survive
no one intimated to me the order of this scalp
it is me
                separated
                        to start again
in an ardent climate of protohuman genesis
in a time of inaccessible spaces
but from this narrow earth
                                overhang
of this frenzy of retiring quicksands
of this pagan germination
                            future language
Earth Earth
                phallic tangle of my roots
venomous clustered fruit
                        syntax of my lymph
mutating roots of men

I deflower this incredible body that re-emerges
inculcate breath in it
            move it
in the image of a just and violent creation
namely
        g e n e s i s
by the cry
    sidereal biology

                        œuf d'infinis
million de possibilités
                            gestation de peuples
                                            de continents
humanité frétillante
                    et voix
m u t a n t
                    j'échappe
                        je survis
personne ne m'a intimé l'ordre de ce scalp
c'est moi
                    séparé
                        pour reprendre
dans un climat ardent de genèse protohumaine
lors d'espaces inabordables
mais de cette terre étroite
                            surplombe
de ce délire des sables mouvants en retraite
de la germination païenne
                    langage futur
Terre Terre
                l'écheveau phallique de mes racines
la grappe vénéneuse
                syntaxe de ma lymphe
racines mutantes d'hommes

je déflore ce corps inouï qui remerge
lui inculque une respiration
            le meus
à l'image d'une création juste et violente
nommément
        g e n è s e
par le cri
        biologie sidérale

this body of mine
        which is going to live
                to spread itself
defend itself
inalterable
        in its first epic

corps mien
        qui va vivre
                se répandre
se défendre
inaltérable
          en sa première geste

V

To My Son Yacine

À mon fils Yacine

To My Son Yacine

My beloved son
I received your letter
You already speak to me like a grown up
you tell me how hard you work at school
and I sense your passion to understand
to drive out obscurity, ugliness
to penetrate the secrets of the great book of life
You are sure of yourself
and without meaning to
you count your wealth
you assure me of your force
as if you said, "Don't worry about me
watch me walk
watch where my steps go
the horizon, the immense horizon out there
it has no secrets for me"
And I imagine you
your beautiful forehead very high
and straight
I imagine your great pride

My beloved son
I received your letter
You say to me
"I think of you
 and I give you my life"
without suspecting
what you are doing to me by saying that
my crazy heart
my head in the stars
and by this word of yours
I no longer doubt

À mon fis Yacine

Mon fils aimé
j'ai reçu ta lettre
Tu me parles déjà comme une grande personne
tu insistes sur tes efforts à l'école
et je sens ta passion de comprendre
de chasser l'obscurité, la laideur
de pénétrer les secrets du grand livre de la vie
Tu es sûr de toi-même
et sans le faire exprès
tu me comptes tes richesses
tu me rassures sur ta force
comme si tu disais : « Ne t'en fais pas pour moi
regarde-moi marcher
regarde où vont mes pas
l'horizon, l'immense horizon là-bas
il n'a pas de secrets pour moi »
Et je t'imagine
ton beau front bien haut
et bien droit
j'imagine ta grande fierté

Mon fils aimé
j'ai reçu ta lettre
Tu me dis :
« Je pense à toi
et je te donne ma vie »
sans soupçonner
ce que tu me fais en disant cela
mon cœur fou
ma tête dans les étoiles
et par ce mot de toi
je n'ai plus peine à croire

that the great Day will arrive
the day when children like you
having become men
will march in giant strides
away from the poverty of the slums
away from hunger, ignorance and sorrow

My beloved son
I received your letter
You yourself wrote the address
you wrote it with assurance
you told yourself, if I write that
papa will receive my letter
and maybe I will get a reply
and you started to imagine the prison
a big house where people are locked up
how many and why?
but then they cannot see the sea
the forest
they cannot work
so that their children can eat
You imagine something evil
something ugly
something that does not make sense
and makes you become sad
or very angry
You also think
those who made prisons
are certainly crazy
and so many other things
Yes my beloved son
this is the way one begins to think
to understand men
to love life
to detest tyrants

que la grande Fête arrivera
celle où des enfants comme toi
devenus hommes
marcheront à pas de géant
loin de la misère des bidonvilles
loin de la faim, de l'ignorance et des tristesses

Mon fils aimé
j'ai reçu ta lettre
Tu as écrit toi-même l'adresse
tu l'as écrite avec assurance
tu t'es dit, si je mets ça
papa recevra ma lettre
et j'aurai peut-être une réponse
et tu as commencé à imaginer la prison
une grande maison où les gens sont enfermés
combien et pourquoi ?
mais alors ils ne peuvent pas voir la mer
la forêt
ils ne peuvent pas travailler
pour que leurs enfants puissent avoir à manger
Tu imagines quelque chose de méchant
de pas beau
quelque chose qui n'a pas de sens
et qui fait qu'on devient triste
ou très en colère
Tu penses encore
ceux qui ont fait les prisons
sont certainement fous
et tant et tant d'autres choses
Oui mon fils aimé
c'est comme ça qu'on commence à réfléchir
à comprendre les hommes
à aimer la vie
à détester les tyrans

and this is the way
that I love you
that I love to think of you
from the depths of my prison

et c'est comme ça
que je t'aime
que j'aime penser à toi
du fond de ma prison

VI

Four Years

Quatre ans

Four Years

    Soon it will be four years
    they tore me from you
        from my friends
                from my people
    they tied me up
        gagged me
                bound my eyes
    they forbid my poems
                my name
    they exiled me to an islet
    of concrete and rust
    they pinned a number
    on the back of my absence
    they forbade
    the books that I love
           the novels
                the music
    and to see you
    a quarter hour a week
    through two gates separated by a corridor
    they were still there
    drinking the blood of our words
    with a stopwatch
    instead of a brain

Quatre ans

Cela fera bientôt quatre ans
on m'arracha à toi
       à mes camarades
             à mon peuple
on me ligota
       bâillonna
             banda les yeux
on interdit mes poèmes
          mon nom
on m'exila dans un îlot
de béton et de rouille
on apposa un numéro
sur le dos de mon absence
on m'interdit
les livres que j'aime
       les nouvelles
           la musique
et pour te voir
un quart d'heure par semaine
à travers deux grilles séparées par un couloir
ils étaient encore là
buvant le sang de nos paroles
un chronomètre
à la place du cerveau

VII

The Signs Are There

Les signes sont là

The Signs Are There

I

The death
which occurred at night
ended up bowing
in front of life
O invincible light
I am still here
keeping myself company
scrutinizing
the curious beast of time

•

In the eyes
the gaze lights up and dies
One moment
and the hourglass bursts
Where does it come from
this perfume of enigma?

•

What descends from heaven
What rises from earth
The merging lines
The meeting point
The hands lost
in the details
of the body to be born

Les signes sont là

I

La mort
survenue la nuit
a fini par s'incliner
devant la vie
Ô lumière invincible
je suis encore là
à me tenir compagnie
à scruter
la bête curieuse du temps

•

Dans les yeux
le regard s'allume et s'éteint
Un moment
et le sablier éclate
D'où vient
ce parfum d'énigme ?

•

Ce qui descend du ciel
Ce qui monte de la terre
Les lignes de fuite
Le point de rencontre
Les mains s'égarent
sur les détails
du corps à naître

•

Behind the mad clouds
this reddening glow
of a sun in labor
Palmyra or Volubilis?
I paint from memory
I write with my eyes closed

•

I need a base
no matter the element
if I could find in man
the fiber to cling to
If my head
were less heavy to carry
If drinking
really helped with forgetting
If love
proved to be prophetic

And if the only base
were just in the if . . .

•

The signs are there
and you pass
dressed
in the same tunic
of washed-out passions
Ruins of the soul

•

Derrière les nuages fous
il y eut ce rougeoiement
d'un soleil en gésine
Palmyre ou Volubilis ?
Je peins de mémoire
J'écris les yeux fermés

•

Il me faut une assise
peu importe dans quel élément
si je pouvais trouver en l'homme
la fibre à laquelle m'agripper
Si ma tête
était moins lourde à porter
Si le verre
aidait vraiment à oublier
Si l'amour
s'avérait enfin prophétique

Et si la seule assise
n'était que dans le si...

•

Les signes sont là
et vous passez
revêtus
de la même tunique
des passions délavées
Ruines de l'âme

how beautiful you seem
in this twilight
that says its name

•

Who suggests the way
and dictates the halting
From where comes
the sparkling water of knowledge?
Unrepentant walkers
watch as the distance grows
between you and your shadows
The most zealous among you
are only fugitives
and your wine skins are already empty
Maybe thirst
will open your eyes

II

Earth is so patient
it awaits its bard
who is a bit late
then presents himself
Beautiful flatterer
he is quickly forgiven
It's because he's a bit musician
and painter putting his hand in the mix
with words
that know the way of the heart
Here he is
intoning with sincere accents
his ancient refrain

comme vous me semblez belles
dans ce crépuscule
qui dit son nom

●

Qui propose le chemin
et dicte les haltes
D'où vient
l'eau pétillante de la connaissance ?
Marcheurs impénitents
voyez comme la distance se creuse
entre vous et vos ombres
Les plus zélés d'entre vous
ne sont que des fuyards
et vos outres sont déjà vides
La soif
vous ouvrira peut-être les yeux

II

La terre est si patiente
Elle attend son chantre
qui tarde un peu
puis se présente
Beau flatteur
il se fait vite pardonner
C'est qu'il est un peu musicien
et peintre mettant la main à la pâte
avec des mots
qui connaissent le chemin du cœur
Le voici
entonnant avec des accents sincères
sa vieille antienne

that the earth pretends
to hear
for the first time

●

Life has a genius
for invaluable offerings
and to receive them from her hand
it is better to be aware
of the intention
of the ceremony's code
of the moral ablutions
to be fulfilled
of unnecessary words
—like those stupid thank you's—
of the delicacy of gesture
and of the worthy reverence
And then
at the time of withdrawing
above all not to rush
like those victors whose only hurry
is to go exhibit their trophy
to the frustrated crowd

●

It is a house
that is ephemeral
only in the gravity of our forgetting
There even objects
have gained
a robust memory
and give us the change
for our wonder

que la terre fait semblant
d'entendre
pour la première fois

•

La vie s'ingénie
aux offrandes inestimées
et pour les recevoir de sa main
mieux vaut être averti
de l'intention
du code de la cérémonie
des ablutions morales
devant être accomplies
des mots de trop
—comme ces stupides merci—
de la délicatesse du geste
et de la révérence digne
Et puis
au moment de se retirer
surtout ne pas se précipiter
comme ces vainqueurs qui n'ont d'autre hâte
que d'aller exhiber à la foule des frustrés
leur trophée

•

C'est une maison
qui n'est éphémère
que par la gravité de nos oublis
Même les objets
y ont acquis
une solide mémoire
et nous rendent la monnaie
de notre émerveillement

if sincere wonder
there were
on our part

•

It is a house
where we have received profusely
the savor and odor of beings
the tactile colors of elements
the modest beauty of trees
We have eaten there by preference
with the stranger
drunk with the most desperate tablemates
and kept awake night and day
with our knowing phantoms
There we have conceived the free infants
of our dreams
All that
while keeping an eager ear to the door
to tune in to the hesitant steps
of the unexpected

•

What have I to ask
of the deployed wing of time
of the black sail of the phantom ship
of the always rotten wheel
of fortune?
What I hold between my hands
suffices as a support
The only coordinate that matters
is this segment of life
traced by the fire

si émerveillement sincère
de notre part
il y a eu

•

C'est une maison
où nous avons reçu à profusion
la saveur et l'odeur des êtres
les couleurs tactiles des éléments
la beauté pudique des arbres
Nous y avons mangé de préférence
avec l'étranger
bu avec le commensal le plus désespéré
et veillé de nuit comme de jour
avec nos fantômes avisés
Nous y avons conçu les enfants libres
de nos rêves
Tout cela
en gardant une oreille suspendue à la porte
pour capter les pas hésitants
de l'inespéré

•

Qu'ai-je à demander
à l'aile déployée du temps
à la voile noire du navire fantôme
à la roue toujours véreuse
de la fortune ?
Ce que je tiens entre les mains
me suffit comme viatique
La seule coordonnée qui vaille
est ce segment de vie
tracé par le feu

that a vestal of my knowledge
never ceases to feed
to my great delight

•

In this burning crucible
I am camping
right down to my Turkish slippers
The inspired fire
gets fanned by the breeze
By some conventional signs
it is spring once again
Love is lit up
by some remembered scents
as on the glorious day of its birth

•

Friendly tempest
grant yourself
grant me respite
The harbor is in sight
I deliver my sides and armpits to you
the two dry raisins of my chest
I entrust you with my lute and flute
Play on me at your convenience
Listen to me as I listen to you
The poem
attracted by so many considerations
clears its throat
and with no more fuss
gives the note *la*

qu'une vestale de ma connaissance
ne cesse d'alimenter
à ma grande joie

•

Dans ce creuset ardent
je campe
droit dans mes babouches
Le feu inspiré
se laisse gagner par la brise
À certains signes convenus
il fait de nouveau printemps
À certains fragrances du souvenir
l'amour s'illumine
comme au jour glorieux de sa naissance

•

Tempête amie
accorde-toi
accorde-moi une accalmie
Le havre est en vue
Je te livre mon flanc et mes aisselles
le deux raisins secs de ma poitrine
Je te confie mon luth et ma flûte
Joue de moi à ta convenance
Écoute-moi que je t'écoute
Le poème
par tant de prévenances alléché
s'éclaircit la voix
et sans plus de manières
donne le *la*

III

The poem
if it is a poem
will always astonish
—that's the least of things—
It is the same with its sister
liberty
There it is!
does she only have a face?
The question is not overrated
One would love to be able to recognize her
even if one were plunged
into any kind of circle of hell
To be assured that she could smile at others
in distant times
and will smile at others again
in a still more distant future
To greet her in passing
with blinking lashes of an eye
that has not faded
To accompany her with the ultimate glimmer
of the pupil that she inflamed
when your belief
was iron clad

•

On the faces dimly lit
I do not need the wrinkle marks
to reread our history
Every smile
has the value and weight
of overwhelming experienced pain
Of cries never uttered

III

Le poème
s'il y a poème
étonnera toujours
—c'est la moindre des choses—
Il en va de même de sa sœur
la liberté
Tenez !
a-t-elle seulement un visage ?
La question n'est pas surfaite
On aimerait pouvoir la reconnaître
même si l'on était plongé
dans je ne sais quel cercle de l'enfer
S'assurer qu'elle a pu sourire à d'autres
en des époques lointaines
et sourira à d'autres encore
dans un plus lointain avenir
La saluer au passage
d'un clignement des cils de l'œil
qui n' s'est pas éteint
L'accompagner avec l'ultime lueur
de la pupille qu'elle a enflammée
quand on y avait cru
dur comme fer

•

Sur les visages faiblement éclairés
je n'ai pas besoin du tracé des rides
pour relire notre histoire
Chaque sourire
a valeur et poids de douleur
vécue et terrassée
Des cris jamais proférés

to disappoint the torturers
Years without horizon
sewn into other years
to create the flag of return
Clandestine poems
formerly etched into the filth of walls
now deposited in the hands
of children and grandchildren of the ordeal
Each smile
has its weight of gold
which makes the scale tilt
to the side of resuscitated memory

•

Among so many victories
ugly and stupefying
the one
so rare
of the vanquished
is and ought to be modest
It is with a few friends
that it is usually celebrated
on fleeting occasions
where the actors who are now
witnesses embrace
slap each other roughly on the back
double over with laughter at the deliverance
and end up raising a glass
to the dear absentees
the distinguished travelers
on the raft of eternity

afin de désespérer les bourreaux
D'années sans horizon
cousues à d'autres années
pour confectionner le drapeau du retour
De poèmes clandestins
jadis gravés dans la crasse des murs
aujourd'hui déposés entre les mains
des enfants et petits-enfants de l'épreuve
Chaque sourire
a ce pesant d'or
qui fait pencher la balance
du côté de la mémoire ressuscitée

•

Parmi tant de victoires
laides et abrutissantes
celle
si rare
des vaincus
est et se doit d'être modeste
C'est en petit comité
qu'elle est d'habitude célébrée
en des occasions fugaces
où les acteurs
devenus témoins s'embrassent
en se donnant de rudes tapes dans le dos
se tordent du rire de la délivrance
et finissent par lever leur verre
aux chers absents
voyageurs émérites
sur le radeau de l'éternité

•

The gaping crater
dug by absence
that memory has difficulty filling
First it is the voice that is missed
even before the face
and the rippling palette
We cling then to any gesture
any figure free of gait
to the fetish words and the tics of language
to a shared surprise pizza
at the moment of evening call to prayer
to exchanged advice
on the right place for bread
for coffee
or for paper

How does one sculpt the living
with the anarchic material of death?

    —for Mohammed Kacimi. In memoriam

•

Of course
there will be the skeptic of the service
the menacing look and the clammy hands
He will snicker
at the sight of his neighbor's tears
and will rejoice *in petto*
having had a narrow escape
At the end of the ceremony
he will applaud weakly
then to the fervent ones

•

Le cratère béant
creusé par l'absence
et que le souvenir peine à combler
C'est d'abord la voix qui manque
avant même le visage
et sa palette ondoyante
On se raccroche alors à tel geste
telle figure libre de la démarche
à des mots fétiches ou des tics de langage
à une pizza-surprise partagée
au moment de l'appel à la prière du soir
à des conseils échangés
sur la bonne adresse du pain
du café
ou du papier

Ah comment sculpter le vivant
avec la matière anarchique de la mort ?

—*à Mohammed Kacimi. In memoriam*

•

Bien sûr
il y aura le sceptique de service
l'œil torve et les mains moites
Il ricanera
à la vue des larmes de la voisine
et jouira in petto
de l'avoir échappé belle
Au terme de la cérémonie
il applaudira du bout des doigts
puis à l'adresse des fervents

making a circle around the leader
he will launch from afar
his inaudible and unstoppable
yes . . . but

•

Fortunately the writings are there
so there is no need to repeat oneself
or seek to convince the incredulous
Outlets and porters
they allow us to breathe
the time that a new concern
arises
and puts an end to the lull
It is fortunate that the writings remain
if only for a moment
And now
friendly tempest
whenever you wish

faisant cercle autour de l'officiant
il lancera de loin
son inaudible et imparable
oui... mais

•

Heureusement que les écrits sont là
pour que l'on n'ait pas à se répéter
ou chercher à convaincre l'incrédule
Exutoires et portefaix
il nous permettent de souffler
le temps qu'une nouvelle inquiétude
se dresse
et mette un terme à l'accalmie
Heureusement que les écrits restent
ne serait-ce qu'un moment
Et maintenant
tempête amie
quand tu voudras

VIII

The Poem Under Gag (i)

Sous le bâillon le poème (i)

The Poem Under Gag

Hello sunshine of my country
how good it is to be alive today
so much light
so much light around me
Hello wasteland of my walk
you've become familiar to me
I pace briskly
and you fit me like an elegant shoe
Hello philosophical oxpecker oaf bird
tickling your ribs
with small distracted pecks
perched on that wall
that hides the world from me
Hello stunted weeds of the alleyway
shivering with small opalescent wrinkles
under the teasing caress of the wind
Hello big lonely palm tree
planted on your shaggy stilt
and opening at your crown
like a splendid tulip
Hello sunshine of my country
tide of presence annihilating exile
So much light
so much light around me

•

I have a thousand reasons to live
to defeat the daily death
the happiness of loving you
marching in step with hope
We need all our intelligence

Sous le bâillon le poème

Bonjour soleil de mon pays
qu'il fait bon vivre aujourd'hui
que de lumière
que de lumière autour de moi
Bonjour terrain vague de ma promenade
tu m'es devenu familier
je t'arpente vivement
et tu me vas comme un soulier élégant
Bonjour pique-bœuf balourd et philosophe
perché là-haut
sur cette muraille qui me cache le monde
te chatouillant les côtes
à petits coups distraits
Bonjour herbe chétive de l'allée
frissonnant en petites rides opalescentes
sous la caresse taquine du vent
Bonjour grand palmier solitaire
planté sur ton échasse grenue
et t'ouvrant comme une splendide tulipe
à la cime
Bonjour soleil de mon pays
marée de présence annihilant l'exil
Que de lumière
que de lumière autour de moi

•

J'ai mille raisons de vivre
vaincre la mort quotidienne
le bonheur de t'aimer
marcher au pas de l'espoir
Nous avons besoin de toute notre intelligence

for failure
disillusionment
stubborn facts that corrode
the dreams of naivety
the path shortens
with this new lucidity

•

To learn silence
so that our words weigh
with all their burden of suffering
To tell the quintessence of our acts
Under the headband of the executioner
to know how to detect the banner
of our self-importance

•

Faced with time
memory
ebbs and flows
The present does not exist
unless you call the present
this acute awareness
of becoming
which strikes down the past

•

So many years
Of never having known
loneliness or boredom
So many shooting stars in my head
The bath of tenderness

pour l'échec
la désillusion
les faits têtus qui corrodent
les rêves de naïveté
et de cette nouvelle lucidité
le chemin s'écourte

•

Apprendre le silence
pour que nos paroles pèsent
de tout leur poids de souffrance
Dire la quintessence de nos actes
Sous le bandeau du bourreau
savoir déceler le bandeau
de notre propre suffisance

•

Aux prises avec le temps
la mémoire
flux et reflux
Le présent n'existe pas
à moins d'appeler présent
cette conscience aiguë
du devenir
foudroyant le passé

•

Tant d'années
à n'avoir jamais connu
la solitude ou l'ennui
tant d'étoiles filantes dans ma tête
La vasque de tendresse murmure

during a song
whispers the strange happiness of the prisoner

•

Night has let loose its horde of doves
in the sensual forests of memory
You appear to me
terrifying with grace and promises
then it is the rite
interspersed with detonations
of jeering voyeurs whose masks stink
I am only half a man

•

Water flows in my hand
Iridescent droplets
greedily absorb the sun
To dream is only the reflection
of this near miracle

•

The smile blossoms by itself
I do not tear it from my face
forgotten along with all the mirrors
Inextinguishable smile
this is how I resist

•

The comrades are sleeping
Prison has stopped swirling in their heads
They sail with an open heart

en plein chant
l'étrange bonheur du prisonnier

•

La nuit a lâché sa horde de colombes
sur les forêts sensuelles du souvenir
Tu m'apparais
terrifiante de grâces et de promesses
puis c'est le rite
entrecoupé de détonations
de voyeurs hilares puant la cagoule
Je ne suis qu'à moitié homme

•

L'eau coule dans ma main
Des gouttelettes irisées
absorbent goulûment le soleil
Rêver n'est que le reflet
de ce presque miracle

•

Le sourire éclôt de lui-même
Je ne l'arrache pas à ma face
oubliée avec tous les miroirs
Sourire inextinguible
c'est comme ça que je résiste

•

Les camarades dorment
La prison a cessé de tournoyer dans leur tête
Ils naviguent à cœur ouvert

on the high sea of our unexpressed passions
They are beautiful in their sleep

•

Every day
this blank page that taunts me
as if declaring the victory of silence
A thousand poems burst under the everyday rubble
The perverse times reeling out the words to say them

•

Still far off is the time of cherries
and of hands loaded with instant offerings
the open skies of fresh mornings of freedom
the speaking with joy
and the happy sadness

Still far off is the time of cherries
and cities made marvelous with silence
at the fragile dawn of our loves
the ravenous encountering
the crazy dreams become daily tasks

Still far off is the time of cherries
but I already feel it
throbbing and rising
all hot in seed
with my future passion

•

I'm doing fine
I tell you

en haute mer de nos passions inédites
Ils sont beaux dans leur sommeil

●

Chaque jour
cette page blanche qui me nargue
comme pour décréter la victoire du silence
Mille poèmes éclatés sous les décombres du quotidien
Les temps pervers dévidant les mots pour les dire

●

C'est loin le temps des cerises
et des mains chargées d'offrandes immédiates
le ciel ouvert au matin frais des libertés
la joie de dire
et la tristesse heureuse

C'est encore loin le temps des cerises
et des cités émerveillées de silence
à l'aurore fragile de nos amours
la fringale des rencontres
les rêves fous devenus tâches quotidiennes

C'est encore loin le temps des cerises
mais je le sens déjà
qui palpite et lève
tout chaud en germe
dans ma passion du futur

●

Ça va très bien
je vous le dis

Do not laugh
> don't doubt it at all

Hope
> is serious

when it is rational
Of course it's not an army
a magic wand
but it is a sure guide
an excellent dowser
Believe me
there's room for hope

—Maison centrale de Kénitra, 1978

Ne riez pas
            ne doutez point
L'espoir
     c'est sérieux
quand il est rationnel
Bien sûr ce n'est pas une armée
une baguette magique
mais c'est un guide sûr
un excellent sourcier
Croyez-moi
il y a lieu d'espoir

—Maison centrale de Kénitra, 1978

IX

The Last Poem of Jean Sénac

Le dernier poème de Jean Sénac

The Last Poem of Jean Sénac

He did not shut himself in to write
his poem sensed danger
left him the open door
No poem without risk
His beard smoothed the pubis
of the transparent page
and his lips were murmuring
the surah of forgiveness
He first drew a sun
a small schoolboy circle
decked out with disproportionate rays
The night was screaming rape
Algiers was drinking itself to death
among men
Then he cut his pencil
or slashed his vein
but I imagine
he wrote in red
without erasures
the following fragments:

"Shipwrecked fingers
sculpted in silence
Other suffocations arise
from the bitter neck of speech
All this vomit of nothings
at the entrance of the poem
The words are not lacking
rather
the will to say it
To what good
to what bad?

Le dernier poème de Jean Sénac

Il ne s'est pas enfermé pour écrire
son poème a flairé le danger
lui a laissé la porte ouverte
Pas de poème sans risque
Sa barbe lissait le pubis
de la page transparente
et ses lèvres murmuraient
la sourate du pardon
Il dessina d'abord un soleil
un petit rond d'écolier
affublé de rayons démesure
La nuit criait au viol
Alger buvait à mort
entre hommes
Puis il tailla son crayon
ou se taillada une veine
mais j'imagine
qu'il écrivit au rouge
sans ratures
les fragments que voici :

« Naufrage des doigts
sculptés dans le silence
D'autres suffocations montent
du goulot amer du dire
Tous ces riens vomis
sur le parvis du poème
Les mots ne manquent pas
plutôt
le vouloir dire
À quoi bon
à quoi mauvais ?

Pain
only

The poem that does not want to be born
has its reasons

Above all
not to beg
at the gate of silence
but to manage it
like a grand text

It is we
who have aged
not the world

I ate
one after the other
my little illusions
As for the large ones
I keep them
so like jewels
they can permanently illuminate
my burial
Why do I feel guilty
when happiness invades me?

Fortunately there is the sea
blue-gray in its greenness gorged with seagulls
a jubilant boat we do not know
at the water's bottom or in the hem of clouds
Fortunately there is the openness
holding the breath of the earth
and the dripping wind slipping through caressing foliage
Fortunately man can see himself

La douleur
seule

Le poème qui ne veut pas naître
a ses raisons

Surtout
ne pas mendier
à la porte du silence
mais le gérer
comme un grand texte

C'est nous
qui avons vieilli
pas le monde

J'ai mangé
l'une après l'autre
mes petites illusions
Quant aux grandes
je me les garde
pour qu'elles éclairent durablement
ma sépulture
tels des joyaux
Pourquoi je me sens coupable
quand le bonheur m'envahit ?

Heureusement qu'il y a la mer
bleu-gris de son vert gorgé de mouettes
une barque jubilant on ne sait
au fond de l'eau ou dans l'ourlet des nuages
Heureusement qu'il y a ce large
retenant le souffle de la terre
et le vent coulis ondoyant de frondaisons câlines
Heureusement que l'homme peut se voir

smile at his distant look alike
elsewhere than in mirrors

Nothing I learned
helped me
to tear the hymen of your eyes
serene tree of perennial sap
that will once more irrigate me
when my buried mouth turns off in the sands

I am born
to love
hate is a stranger to me

Happy people
do not have poetry"

The door closed
The odorless shadow
appeared on the threshold
The knife cut the sun in two
before penetrating
the sacred womb
of breath

Sénac had raised his head
he looked into eyes
of whoever came first
laughed
as he always did
and handed out his last poem

sourire à son lointain sosie
autrement que dans les miroirs

Rien de ce que j'ai appris
ne m'a servi
à déchirer l'hymen de tes yeux
arbre serein de sève pérenne
qui m'irriguera encore
quand ma bouche s'éteindra dans les sables

Je suis né
pour aimer
la haine m'est étrangère

Les peuples heureux
n'ont pas de poésie »

La porte s'est refermée
L'ombre sans odeur
apparut sur le seuil
Le couteau a fendu le soleil en deux
avant de pénétrer
dans l'enceinte sacrée
du souffle

Sénac avait levé la tête
il regardait dans les yeux
riait
comme il en avait l'habitude
en tendant au premier venu
son dernier poème

X

Pastures of Silence

Pâturages du silence

Pastures of Silence

I

Lift up your pain
and walk
As long as the earth turns
hope remains
to touch the slaves
who carry on their shoulders
the abandoned vault of heaven

•

Do not divert
from the stations of the cross
The tree of knowledge
will loom
like a meteorite
thundering dismay
Then you will know
that suffering
is the diastole
and systole
of any essential quest

•

Question
and burn with your questions
Affirm nothing
that is not
marked with the blood
of your furious concern for truth

Pâturages du silence

I

Soulève ta douleur
et marche
Tant que cette terre tourne
il reste l'espoir
d'émouvoir les esclaves
qui portent sur leurs épaules
la voûte désaffectée du ciel

•

Sur le chemin de croix
ne te détourne pas
L'arbre de la connaissance
surgira
tel une météorite
foudroyant le désarroi
Alors tu sauras
que la souffrance
est la diastole
et la systole
de toute quête essentielle

•

Interroge
et brûle à tes interrogations
N'affirme rien
qui ne soit
marqué jusqu'au sang
de ta furie inquiète de vérité

•

Do not write
do not write anything
before you feel mounting
from your most distant roots
the sap of the song
that your small bard-like body
won't be able to contain
under pain of immolation

•

If the chains keep you from walking
keep your eyes open
If your crippled neck stops you
from raising your head
keep your eyes open
If they close your eyes forcefully
reopen them
in the seismic continent
of your body

•

Nothing in the world
will oblige you
to surrender
to renounce
your human identity
Do not gauge your strength
by the measure of your executioner

•

N'écris pas
n'écris rien
avant de sentir monter en toi
et du plus loin de tes racines
la sève du chant
que ton petit corps d'aède
ne pourra plus contenir
sous peine d'immolation

•

Si les chaînes t'empêchent de marcher
garde les yeux ouverts
Si ta nuque percluse
t'empêche de lever la tête
garde les yeux ouverts
Si on te ferme les yeux de force
rouvre-les
dedans le continent sismique
de ton corps

•

Rien au monde
ne pourra t'obliger
à plier genou
renoncer
à ton identité humaine
Ne mesure pas ta force
à la balance de tes bourreaux

•

My very sweet earth
they call you
"infested by men"
and your long journey
a simple parenthesis
in the infernal swaying of the world
My very sweet earth
daughter of our love

•

This heritage is heavy
this unwritten testament
of those condemned
to existence who bequeath you
the key of their voice
from their imperishable smile
enveloping the fabulous walk
at the zenith of which
they were slain
by snipers

•

Abrupt word
my seasoned nomad ark
to dig the labyrinth
through unbearable nights
from months to years to whirling centuries
in the lavish jungle
Abrupt night
door of my exodus
loaded

•

Terre ma douce
on te dit
« infestée d'hommes »
et ton périple
une simple parenthèse
dans le roulis infernal du monde
Terre ma douce
fille de notre amour

•

Lourd cet héritage
ce testament non écrit
des condamnés de l'existence
que te lèguent
la clé de leur voix
de leur sourire inextinguible
enveloppant la marche fabuleuse
au zénith de laquelle
ils furent abattus
par des tireurs d'élite

•

Abrupte parole
mon arche de nomade aguerri
par insoutenables nuits
à creuser le labyrinthe
de mois en années en siècles de tournoiement
dedans la jungle prodiguée
Abrupte nuit
porte de mon exode
richissime

despite this fire of roots
illuminating the earth

•

Men have really changed
old convict laborers of splendid dreams
This one who talks to you about comfort
as a right of maturity
Another keeps eyes on you with a messy tenderness
so that you share with him
the daily inebriation
the dust of time
Another again
eyeing bluntly
your surgical virginity
warms up his good conscience
with the exorbitant fire
of your shyness
And the other who draws morals
from both rain and good weather
stops you in the street
probes you down to the entrails
with a mathematical look
and with his carnivorous and small humid hand
tells you the right way
while rubbing circles on his arm

•

Everything is dead they say
and in bulk the amalgam
God   Man   Love
hope in the teen museum
the people slouched at the foot of the thrones

malgré ce feu de racines
illuminant la terre

•

Les hommes ont bien changé
vieux forçat des rêves splendides
Celui-là qui te parle du confort
comme un droit de la maturité
Un autre te couve d'une tendresse malpropre
pour que tu partages avec lui
la cuite quotidienne
la poussière de temps
Un autre encore
lorgne sans ambages
ta virginité chirurgicale
se réchauffe la bonne conscience
au feu exorbitant
de ta timidité
Et l'autre qui tire morale
de la pluie et du beau temps
t'arrête dans la rue
te sonde jusqu'aux entrailles
d'un regard mathématique
et de sa menotte carnassière et humide
t'indique le droit chemin
en imprimant un geste circulaire à son bras

•

Tout est mort dit-on
et en vrac l'amalgame
Dieu   l'Homme   l'Amour
l'espoir au musée d'adolescence
les peuples avachis au pied des trônes

of their slouching potentates
the amnesiac workers
delighting themselves in their chains
the youth populating
artificial paradises
the women spokespersons
of their millennial silence
the Third World getting in touch again
with the golden age of barbarities
Everything is dead they say
but what then is this rumor
which rises from cemeteries
Would the dead be more talkative
that the living?

•

Dawn
restores your transparency
Here you are standing
rich in your nudity
at a loss
as if for the first time
before the heart and the body of the beloved
after years of separation
All your enemies have disappeared
nothing remains
but the enemies of dawn

II

Take out your hands
spread them to the great sun of fecundations

de leurs potentats avachis
les ouvriers amnésiques
se délectant de leurs chaînes
la jeunesse peuplant
les paradis artificiels
les femmes porte-parole
de leur silence millénaire
le tiers-monde renouant
avec l'âge d'or des barbaries
Tout est mort dit-on
mais quelle est donc cette rumeur
qui monte des cimetières
Les morts seraient-ils plus bavards
que les vivants ?

•

L'aurore
te restitue ta transparence
Te voilà debout
riche de ta nudité
désemparé
comme pour la première fois
devant le cœur et le corps de la bien-aimée
après des années de séparation
Tous tes ennemis ont disparu
il ne reste plus
que les ennemis de l'aurore

II

Sors tes mains
étale-les au grand soleil des fécondations

reread the map of your palms
observe your wrist
until you can feel the pulsations in it
Each beat will release a seed
Now shake yourself
Here comes the time
when you must take up again
your work as seed sower

•

The eyes of the martyrs
do not look alike
There are some which reflect
sadness or joy
Others who express
disarray or serenity
The eyes of the martyrs
stay eternally open
vast constellation
showing the shepherds of the human night
the steep hub
of the hidden face of earth

•

While poetry agonizes
in the convulsions of the last one
crazy with love
and while the reign of barbarity envelops
the last monuments of our fragility
While the dinosaurs
pierce the shell of atavistic drowsiness
and spread among the ruins of our hands
While the cooling of the planet

relis la carte de tes paumes
observe ton poignet
jusqu'à ce que t'en apparaissent les pulsations
Chaque battement libérera une graine
Maintenant ébroue-toi
Voici venir le temps
où tu dois reprendre
ton métier de semeur

•

Les yeux des martyrs
ne se ressemblent pas
Il y en a qui reflètent
la tristesse ou la joie
D'autres qui expriment
e désarroi ou la sérénité
Les yeux des martyrs
restent éternellement ouverts
vaste constellation
indiquant aux bergers de la nuit humaine
l'abrupt pôle
de la face cachée de la terre

•

Tandis que la poésie agonise
dans les convulsions du dernier
fou d'amour
et que le règne de barbarie enveloppe
les derniers monuments de notre fragilité
Tandis que les dinosauriens
percent la coquille de l'atavique somnolence
et se répandent parmi les ruines de nos mains
Tandis que la refroidissement de la planète

grievously reaches the heart of man
and the few survivors emigrate
panicking
toward a hypothetical equator
While the tears of stone
blur my sight . . .
No
I don't want to believe it

•

I open the windows wide
I welcome
the epic silence
The terrible rumor
pierces my skull
gets through
I stagger in the turbulence
of the sneering wind
hang on to my books
onto the guitar of the beloved
with a two-way mirror
where I plunge my head
into the sunbeam that refracts
in my cup of coffee
and I rise up again
having grabbed by the horns
the minotaur of silence

•

This voice which rises
from my common memory
and which rumbles
with each accession of my body

atteint grièvement le cœur de l'homme
et que les rares survivants émigrent
paniquement
vers un hypothétique équateur
Tandis que des larmes de pierre
brouillent ma vue...
Non
je ne veux pas y croire

•

J'ouvre toutes grandes les fenêtres
J'accueille
le silence épique
La terrible rumeur
vrille mon crâne
traverse
je titube dans le tourbillon
du vent ricanant
m'accroche aux livres
à la guitare de l'Aimée
aux miroir sans tain
où je plonge la tête
au rayon de soleil qui réfracte
dans ma tasse de café
et je me relève
ayant empoigné par les cornes
le minotaure du silence

•

Cette voix qui monte
de ma mémoire générique
et qui gronde
dans chaque avènement de mon corps

This voice is more and more strangled
in my narrow envelope
This voice of always
and of everywhere
of fluttering shrouds of life
of all aphasias
of all amnesias
This voice
that I sometimes do not dare
call mine

•

The well-known cell
that I carry in my head
The small yard for walking
that I carry in my feet
The big keys of big locks
which turn and slam
still every day
within my chest
The striped grey uniform
that grew back
under my clothes of skin
The eyes of my friends
laid into my eyes
with which I scrutinize
the theater of shadows
of freedom day by day

•

Loving you is so good
Adwah
and so hard

Cette voix de plus en plus étranglée
dans mon enveloppe étroite
Cette voix de toujours
et de partout
des suaires palpitant de vie
de toutes les aphasies
de toutes les amnésies
Cette voix
que je n'ose parfois
appeler mienne

•

La cellule familière
que je transporte dans ma tête
La petite cour de promenade
que je transporte dans mes pieds
Les grosses clés des grosses serrures
qui tournent et claquent
quotidiennement encore
dans ma poitrine
L'uniforme gris rayé
qui a repoussé
sous mes habits de peau
Les yeux de mes camarades
incrustés dans les yeux
avec lesquels je scrute
le théâtre d'ombres
de la liberté à la petite semaine

•

T'aimer est si bon
Awdah
et si dur

Now
I feel fully like a man
and that is exactly why
my quest
becomes more painful

•

The torturer has awakened
Near him
his wife is still sleeping
He slips furtively out of bed
puts on his jungle outfit
and goes out
On the way to the shed
where his instruments and the victims
of the day await him
he thinks of ordinary things of life
rising prices
the house that will be too small
when the fifth child arrives
the rains that are late again this year
the end of the last episode of the tv show
He clocks in at the entry desk
heads toward the shed
opens the door
The bodies are huddled in the dark
the rasps
the stench
Get up, you son of a bitch!
he yells
giving a mule kick
to the gut of the first accused
his foot meets

Maintenant
je me sens pleinement homme
et c'est pour cela justement
que ma quête
devient plus douloureuse

•

Le tortionnaire s'est réveillé
Près de lui
sa femme dort encore
Il se glisse furtivement hors du lit
revêt sa tenue de jungle
et sort
Sur le chemin du réduit
où l'attendent ses instruments
et ses victimes du jour
il pense aux choses ordinaires de la vie
les prix qui grimpent
la maison qui sera trop exiguë
quand viendra le cinquième enfant
les pluies qui tardent de nouveau cette année
le dénouement du dernier feuilleton qui passe à la télé
Il pointe au bureau des entrées
se dirige vers le réduit
ouvre la porte
Les corps sont recroquevillés dans la pénombre
toussotements
puanteur
Lève-toi fils de pute !
crie-t-il
en lançant une ruade
au plexus du premier prévenu
que son pied rencontre

•

We separated you
when she was barely six
Here she comes slouching on your bed
her chest swollen with fruit stolen
from the garden of the Hesperides
eyes of a gazelle
grazing in an oasis
forbidden to hunters
She talks to you about the miseries of school
tells you
"to keep in confidence"
that she has a boyfriend
And here you are not knowing how
you catch yourself saying to her
"Give me back my little girl!"

•

[Why did the androgynes
rebel against the gods
Did they not thus have the intuition
that the separation to be inflicted on them
would open the way
to the quest
which will mark irreversibly
our human condition?]

•

Write
write as fast as you can
as long as the hot flow
has not cooled down

•

On vous a séparés
lorsqu'elle avait à peine six ans
La voilà qui vient s'affaler sur ton lit
la poitrine gonflée de fruits volés
au jardin des Hespérides
les yeux d'une gazelle
broutant dans une oasis
interdite aux chasseurs
Elle te parle des misères de l'école
t'informe
« pour garder ta confiance »
qu'elle a un petit ami
Et voilà que tu ne sais comment
tu te surprends à lui dire :
« Rends-moi ma petite fille » !

•

[Pourquoi les androgynes
se sont-ils révoltés contre les dieux
N'avaient-ils pas ainsi l'intuition
que la séparation qui leur sera infligée
ouvrira la voie
à la quête
qui marquera irréversiblement
notre humaine condition ?]

•

Écris
écris aussi vite que tu peux
tant que la coulée vive
ne s'est pas refroidie

as long as the volcano
tears out its guts
before finding
the peace of the dead
Otherwise
your word would just be junk
pieces of glass without a kaleidoscope
the horseshit of an insomniac

•

When you reread yourself
respect your word
Do not take out the scalpel
of your intellectual tics
Do not cut the buds
from the still-born leaves
But be an intelligent reader
a demanding
and compassionate man
Be careful
to not strangle
your strange Doppleganger

•

Your pain is not the end of the world
Plunge into the tablecloth where it originates
[make a chart of it]
the tributaries and inflows
go up and down all the streams
Like the navigators
you will end up no longer being seasick
You will know
that any sea is provisionary

tant que le volcan
se déchire les entrailles
avant de retrouver
la paix des morts
Autrement
ta parole ne serait que pacotille
verroterie sans kaléidoscope
crottin d'insomniaque

•

Quand tu te relis
respecte ta parole
Ne sors pas le bistouri
de tes tics intellectuels
Ne coupe pas les bourgeons
d'avec les feuilles mort-nées
Mais sois lecteur intelligent
homme d'exigence
et de compassion
Prends garde
à ne pas stranguler
ton étrange sosie

•

Ta douleur n'es pas la fin du monde
Plonge dans la nappe où elle prend source
[dresse-en la carte]
des influents et des confluents
remonte et descends tous les cours
Comme les navigateurs
tu finiras par ne plus avoir le mal de mer
Tu sauras
que toute mer est provisoire

•

[Who are we?
mutants of the lab of History
irredentist nomads
parked on the reserves
of the contagious zinc
crazed by daily heat strokes
of inspired desert pastures
lyricists of the swan song
and the mortal phoenix?
Who are we?
readers of the mirage of the sands
inanimate scribes
on the table of the old commandments
allegory of the impossible?
Who are we?
until when shall we carry
that question
this cross
this prisoner's ball and chain
of our own body?]

•

When Sheherazade stopped talking
at the dawn of the thousand and first night
and recognized the pains of childbirth
she cried for the first time
The sword of Shahrayar
no longer hung over her head
but the door of the harem
closed itself behind her
She knew she had crossed the threshold
of her endless agony

•

[Qui sommes-nous ?
mutants du laboratoire de l'Histoire
irrédentistes nomades
parqués dans les réserves
du zinc contagieux
fous d'insolations diurnes
des pâturages du désert inspiré
paroliers du chant du cygne
et du phénix mortel ?
Qui sommes-nous ?
liseurs du mirage des sables
scribes inanimés
sur la table des vieux commandements
allégorie de l'impossible ?
Qui sommes-nous ?
jusqu'à quand porterons-nous
cette question
cette croix
ce boulet de prisonniers
de notre propre corps ?]

•

Lorsque Shéhérazade se tut
à l'aube de la mille et unième nuit
et qu'elle reconnut les douleurs de l'enfantement
elle pleura pour la première fois
L'épée de Shahrayar
n'était plus suspendue sur sa tête
mais la porte du harem
se refermait derrière elle
Elle sut qu'elle avait enjambé le seuil
de son interminable agonie

•

Meanwhile
Al-Hallaj loudly laughed
in the delirium of his pyre
and some thought they heard him whisper:
"Poor you
my brothers
you are burning
the only parchment
of the secret of your strength"

•

At that precise moment
Al Maârri regained his eyesight
He was surprised to discover
that hell
was not a mere promise
The desert was a vast blaze
ordained by the Masters of the hour
to exterminate the race of schismatic cameleers
and the imposter babbling poets
Here comes the era of grand Silence
Al Maârri said
and he closed his eyes again
to better contemplate
the dawn
of the great Arab fury

•

From ruse to ruse
stepmother History
pushes the stubborn rock

●

Pendant ce temps
Al-Hallaj s'esclaffait
dans le délire de son bûcher
et d'aucuns crurent l'entendre murmurer :
« Pauvres de vous
mes frères
vous êtes en train de brûler
l'unique parchemin
du secret de votre force »

●

À cet instant précis
Al Maârri recouvra la vue
Il fut surprise de découvrir
que l'enfer
n'était pas une simple promesse
Le désert était un vaste brasier
décrété par les Maîtres de l'heure
pour exterminer la race de chameliers schismatiques
et des poètes imposteurs à la langue pendue
Voici venir l'ère du grand Silence
se dit Al Maârri
et il referma les yeux
pour mieux contempler
l'aube
de la grande colère arabe

●

De ruse en ruse
la marâtre Histoire
pousse le roc têtu

of enlightening ordeals
The world rolls on
through the heartbreaking harrow of holocausts
Tyrannies pass
with short-sighted hopes
But contemplate this prodigy:
every day
millions of newborns
don't hesitate to come out
from the long tunnel of their genesis

III

From the sea to the stars
just a span of tears
Birth of the world
in this fragile stare
that judges the ephemeral
while the rolling of time
plucks the bad weeds
of despair

•

Love sings the old song
of the rupture in all things
traversing mirrors
toward the only earth
where thirst
is still a cardinal virtue

des épreuves éclairantes
Le monde roule sa bosse
sur la herse déchirante des holocaustes
Les tyrannies passent
avec les espoirs à courte vue
Mais contemplez ce prodige :
chaque jour
des millions de nouveau-nés
n'hésitent pas à sortir
du long tunnel de leur genèse

III

De la mer aux étoiles
juste un empan de larmes
Genèse du monde
en ce regard fragile
qui toise l'éphémère
alors que le roulis du temps
arrache les mauvaises herbes
du désespoir

•

De la brisure en toute chose
Amour cantilène
traversant les miroirs
vers l'unique terre
où la soif
est encore vertu cardinale

•

Hubris of this word
that I wreathe like a bridge
To-and-fro of joy
listening to our transparencies
surrendering to goodness
What to say to abolish
the need to talk?

•

Solitude is not a flaw
that must be hidden
with a leaf from a vine
of greedy speeches
When I feel lonely
it is with compassion
for all solitudes

•

Blessed weariness
which arms me against
the intolerance of ideas
which reveals to me
the poison that the statues distill
which directs
my enlightened blind man's cane
in the minefield
where sweet death
feasts
on violent life

•

Orgueil de cette parole
que j'enguirlande comme passerelle
Va-et-vient d'allégresse
écoute de nos transparences
abandon à la bonté
Que dire pour abolir
le besoin de parler ?

•

La solitude n'est pas une tare
qu'il faille cacher
avec la feuille de vigne
des discours cupides
Quand je me sens seul
c'est de compassion
pour toutes les solitudes

•

Inquiétude bénie
qui m'arme
contre l'intolérance des idées
me révèle
le poison que distillent les statues
dirige
ma canne d'aveugle illuminé
dans le champ de mines
où la mort douce
se repaît
de la vie violente

I invite you to transparency
I invite you to the moment of truth
What is the value of a life like ours
I am asking you
Observe the infinity of constellations
observe the long progression
of our intelligent species
dive into the endless labyrinth
of mankind
but finally meditate
stop the infernal machine
of accumulation
shatter the time
of progress without memory
remember your infallible injury
accept this small lot of disorder
Like this
let's fly to rescue the future

•

—And I hear the cry of man—
on earth as in heaven
hoarse
white hot
From crypts where the missing
await the Promise
From delirious bellies
no longer having ears
for any justice
from centuries of centuries
From women beaten—to the soul—to death
confusing the venomous sun
with the red mark
of the final plague

Je vous invite à la transparence
je vous invite à l'instant de vérité
Que vaut une vie comme la nôtre
je vous le demande
Observez l'infini des constellations
observez le long cheminement
de notre espèce intelligente
plongez dans le dédale sans issue
de l'homme
mais méditez enfin
arrêtez la machine infernale
de l'accumulation
brisez le temps
du progrès sans mémoire
souvenez-vous de votre infaillible blessure
acceptez ce petit lot de désarroi
Tels
volons au secours du futur

•

—Et j'entends le cri de l'homme—
sur terre comme au ciel
rauque
chauffé à blanc
De cryptes où les disparus
attendent la Promesse
De ventres déliriels
n'ayant plus d'oreilles
à aucune justice
dans les siècles des siècles
De femmes battues—à l'âme—à mort
confondant le soleil vénéneux
avec la marque rouge
de la peste finale

—and I hear the cry of man—
apocalypse or not

•

Between two nightmares
I dreamed
of a strange and familiar
planet
Everything was music there
elements, men, fauna, flora
She was rolling
the scoundrel
from galaxy to galaxy
leaving lengthily in space
her impressive wake of harmonies
And I was sure
that multiple forms of life
hatched
here and there
everywhere
where my planet had passed
So I decided
in my sleep
not to wake up anymore

•

Amaze yourself
that I can beat the measure
otherwise than in general alarm
fulminating the holy wrath
This is only the first casting
from my volcano of tenderness

—et j'entends le cri de l'homme—
apocalypse ou pas

•

Entre deux cauchemars
j'ai rêvé
d'une étrange et familière
planète
Tout y était musique
éléments, hommes, faune, flore
Elle roulait
la gredine
de galaxie en galaxie
laissant longuement dans l'espace
son impressionnante traîne d'harmonies
Et j'avais la certitude
que de multiples formes de vie
éclosaient
par-ci par-là
partout
où ma planète était passée
Alors je décidai
dans mon sommeil
de ne plus me réveiller

•

Etonnez-vous
que je puisse battre la mesure
autrement qu'en tocsin général
fulminant la sainte colère
Ceci n'est que première coulée
de mon volcan de tendresse

•

One love hides another
one anger hides another
one man hides another
From voice to voice
from mirror to mirror
the craving for truth
that will wring me
until the ultimate face-to-face
with my lot in life
and its death pendant

•

All earth vibrates
far from the looming dawn
in the claws of an excessive shadow
Hear the germination of the day
before opening your eyes
onto the pitiful apocalypse
that will carry your song
toward the infernal triangle
from the spinelessness of silence

•

In the dark hours
there always was
this uncompromising word
except for its own silences
when it had to regenerate
in subterranean water tables
from pain in the colors of hope
Blessed word

●

Un amour en cache un autre
une colère en cache une autre
un homme en cache un autre
De voix en voix
de miroir en miroir
la fringale de vérité
qui me tordra
jusqu'au face-à-face ultime
avec mon lot de vie
et son pendant de mort

●

Toute terre vibre
au large de l'aurore surgie
d'entre les serres d'une pénombre démesure
Entends la germination du jour
avant d'ouvrir les yeux
sur la piteuse apocalypse
qui emportera ton chant
vers le triangle maudit
de la veulerie du silence

●

Aux heures sombres
il y a toujours eu
cette parole sans concession
sauf à ses propres silences
quand il lui fallait de régénérer
dans les nappes souterraines
de la douleur aux couleurs de l'espoir
Parole bénie

within all faculties
that keep us awake

•

Daily prison
large, airy
The arbitrary like an old bloodhound
lurking in the recesses
of day and night
Cramped
inside the body
the war of words
on worn impromptu stages
where still is played
with hardly any change
the tragicomedy
of master and slave

•

—*for André Laude*

Scourged with tall crosses of trials
hiccupping at the seat of the world
pulsating from blackberry roots
of your solar identity
there in the blind hole of all jungle
recognized from generic memory
lying upright in the face
of boreal imminence
miracle
"of the word rising from the base of blood
  sparkling in the darkest wind"
Your lips part

d'entre toutes les facultés
qui nous maintiennent en éveil

•

Prison quotidienne
grande, aérée
L'arbitraire comme un vieux limier
tapi dans les recoins
du jour et de la nuit
A l'étroit
dedans le corps
la guerre des mots
sur les tréteaux usés
où se joue encore
sans retouche à peine
la tragi-comédie
du maître et de l'esclave

•

—*à André Laude*

Flagellé de grandes croix d'épreuves
hoquetant à l'assise du monde
palpitant des mûres racines
de ton identité solaire
là dans le trou aveugle de toute jungle
reconnue de mémoire générique
gisant debout
face aux imminences boréales
miracle
« de la parole surgie du socle du sang
étincelle dans le plus noir vent »
Tes lèvres s'entrouvrent

for the cry
of universal compassion
You loosen the mooring
of the lyrical ship
"of the roses of the future
and of urgent words"
and from century to century
you summarize the inscribed earthquakes
in the indelible march of man
you lacerate
"the nap of consciences"
and you decree:
"all pain is transparency!"
Oh I know the reasons for your sobbing joys
I know the reasons for the magnificence of sadness
and when you metamorphose
again and again in
"jasmine and crazy lilac"
when you resurrect
"in the high flourishing of blood"
you reopen the sluices
of the absolute song
you obliterate the nothingness
of the dead made up for passage
and you debark energetically
in the Continent of Gift
poet cursing the chain of maledictions

•

—for Catherine de Seynes and Jean Bazaine

Come back my sweet friends
I will have for you
even simpler words

pour le cri
de l'universelle compassion
Tu lâches les amarres
du bateau lyrique
« des roses de l'avenir
et des parles urgentes »
et de siècle en siècle
tu résumes les séismes inscrits
dans la marche indélébile de l'homme
tu lacères
« la sieste des consciences »
et tu décrètes :
« Toute douleur est transparence ! »
O j'ai lieu du sanglot de tes joies
j'ai lieu de la magnificence de la tristesse
et quand tu te métamorphoses
encore et encore en
« jasmin et lilas fou »
quand tu ressuscites
« dans la haute floraison du sang »
tu rouvres les vannes
du chant absolu
tu terrasses le néant
des morts fardées de passage
et tu débarques énergiquement
dans le Continent du Don
poète maudissant la chaîne des malédictions

•

—*à Catherine de Seynes et Jean Bazaine*

Revenez mes doux amis
J'aurai pour vous
des mots encore plus simples

I will have for you
these roots that I kept for myself
for bad days
of human indifference
I will have for you
this portion
of undisclosed skyline
where I make and unmake
these torrid seasons of saying
where God takes umbrage at my power
I will have for you
the fontanel of my palms
spread over the stars

•

I will tell you my palette
Black scream of warning pulsating the inaudible
solemn White lighting the ephemeral
Yellow honey cloistered in my uvula
pale Blue piercing through transparency
Green irradiating night walks
Red gnawing at sham ideas
Gray depositing on the horizon
the vibrating egg of dawn
Pink of allied winds
staggering the wrinkles of the world
Of words
of poor words
for harnessing the invisible bull from the clouds

J'aurai pour vous
ces racines que je me gardais
pour les mauvais jours
de l'indifférence humaine
J'aurai pour vous
ce pan de ciel
non révélé
où je fais et défais
les saisons torrides du dire
où Dieu prend ombrage de ma puissance
J'aurai pour vous
la fontanelle de mes paumes
étalées sur les étoiles

•

Je vais vous dire ma palette
cri Noir d'alerte saccadant l'inaudible
Blanc solennel dardant l'éphémère
Jaune miel reclus dans ma luette
Bleu blême transperçant la transparence
Vert irradiant les marches nocturnes
Rouge taraudant la pacotille des idées
Gris déposant sur l'horizon
l'œuf vibrant de l'aurore
Rose des vents alliés
soufflant les rides du monde
Des mots
de pauvres mots
pour dompter le taureau invisible des nuées

XI

Flayed Alive—Epilogue

L'écorché vif—Épilogue

Flayed Alive—Epilogue

The Arab poet
sits at his empty desk
about to write his testament
but discovers he has lost
the use of writing
He has forgotten his own poems
and the poems of his ancestors
He wants to scream with rage
but realizes
he has lost the use of speech
Weary of fighting
he prepares to rise
but senses he has lost
the use of his limbs
Death beat him there
where he had to abdicate
before life

L'écorché vif—Épilogue

Le poète arabe
se met devant sa table rase
s'apprête à rédiger son testament
mais il découvre qu'il a perdu
l'usage de l'écriture
Il a oublié ses propres poèmes
et les poèmes de ses ancêtres
Il veut crier de rage
mais se rend compte
qu'il a perdu l'usage de la parole
De guerre lasse
il s'apprête à se lever
mais il sent qu'il a perdu
l'usage de ses membres
La mort l'a précédé
là où il devait abdiquer
devant la vie

XII

Poems Fallen from the Train

Poèmes tombés du train

Poems Fallen from the Train

Tears rise
in the eyes of the Sphinx
so often the riddle killed

•

Water seeks the desert
that flees from it
thirsty water
inconstant desert

•

All wisdom is illusory
blood breaks the balances
takes away the safeguards
man clings
to the fragments of the mirror

•

The bird
we call the dove
does not care about the mess
its song
is not an answer
to the concerns of the ephemeral

•

This light
is not to be described

Poèmes tombés du train

Les larmes montent
aux yeux du sphinx
tant l'énigme a tué

•

L'eau cherche le désert
qui la fuit
soif de l'eau
inconstance du désert

•

Toute sagesse est illusoire
le sang rompt les équilibres
emporte les garde-fous
l'homme s'agrippe
aux écailles du miroir

•

L'oiseau
disons la tourterelle
se moque du désordre
son chant
n'est pas une réponse
aux inquiétudes de l'éphémère

•

Cette lumière
n'est pas à décrire

it is to be drunk
or eaten

•

The rain announces the colors

•

The leaf shakes
or does not live

•

After us
who will come to collect the inheritance
will the desert bloom again?

•

The poem worries
about threats of extermination
it picks up stones
just in case...

•

—Let's imagine!
—You're kidding, the word is obsolete
—Let's reflect!
—Don't waste your time

elle se boit
ou se mange

•

La pluie annonce les couleurs

•

La feuille tremble
ou ne vit pas

•

Après nous
qui viendra recueillir l'héritage
le désert refleurira-t-il ?

•

Le poème s'inquiète
des menaces d'extermination
il ramasse des pierres
au cas où...

•

—Imaginons !
—Vous plaisantez, le mot est tombé en désuétude
—Réfléchissons !
—Ne perdez pas votre temps

•

Caress
that word that caresses
and calls the caresses
not a word
an element
another light of the heart
in prayer

•

Yellow waits for blue
which lingers with green
white smiles
at this ordinary scene
of bitter love

•

Wine is lawful
wood, O companion
you have nothing to forget
it's by drinking that you remember

•

I drink without a second thought
my glass is an enamored apple
she longs
for the sap that disappears
for the stars that escape ceaselessly
like warned gazelles
my glass is a boy gone crazy
with love

•

Caresse
ce mot qui caresse
et appelle les caresses
pas un mot
un élément
une autre lumière du cœur
en prière

•

Le jaune attend le bleu
qui s'attarde avec le vert
le blanc sourit
à cette scène ordinaire
du dépit amoureux

•

Le vin est licite
bois, ô compagnon
tu n'as rien à oublier
c'est en buvant que tu te souviens

•

Je bois sans arrière-pensée
mon verre est un pomme énamourée
elle se languit
de la sève qui se dérobe
des étoiles qui s'échappent sans cesse
comme des gazelles averties
mon verre est un majnoun
d'amour

•

To live in your body
is not easy
it's a haunted house
a minefield
You should be able to rent it
just for vacations

•

That which is beautiful
is so immediately
universally

•

Is it an injustice
if women are more beautiful
than men?

•

Ugliness
in any case
is unjust

•

The blossoming almond tree
does not suffer criticism

•

Habiter son corps
n'est pas aisé
c'est une maison hantée
un champ de mines
Il faudrait pouvoir le louer
juste pour des vacances

•

Ce qui est beau
l'est immédiatement
universellement

•

Est-ce une injustice
si les femmes sont plus belles
que les hommes ?

•

La laideur
en tout cas
est injuste

•

L'amandier en fleur
ne souffre pas la critique

•

If I write
it's to not despise myself

•

Paradise
it's not a bad idea
provided you can bring
contradiction there

•

Any woman who is sleeping
is making love

•

The majesty of the tree
it sits without ruling
without punishing
without levying taxes
without calling the young
under the flags
without consuming a virgin
each night
without having to lie
It is the perfectly just
monarch

•

I really don't mind
sharing your sorrows

•

Si j'écris
c'est pour ne pas me mépriser

•

Le paradis
ce n'est pas une mauvaise idée
à condition de pouvoir y porter
la contradiction

•

Toute femme qui dort
fait l'amour

•

Majesté de l'arbre
il trône sans gouverner
sans sévir
sans prélever d'impôt
sans appeler les jeunes
sous les drapeaux
sans consommer de vierge
chaque nuit
sans devoir mentir
Il est le monarque
parfaitement juste

•

Je veux bien
me charger de vos tristesses

but why should mine
remain foreign to you?

•

If I threw myself
under the wheels of the train
I would feel sorry for you

•

To want the moon
should be
the smallest common denominator

•

Sometimes to read
is to be humiliated for not writing

•

Dew
is nothing but water
but it is a water of love

•

Look at your hands
look at them
you too
you participate in the mystery

mais pourquoi la mienne
devrait-elle vous rester étrangère ?

●

Si je me jetais
sous les roues d'un train
j'aurais vraiment pitié de vous

●

Vouloir la lune
devrait être
le plus petit dénominateur commun

●

Lire parfois
c'est être humilié de ne pas écrire

●

La rosée
ce n'est que de l'eau
mais c'est une eau amoureuse

●

Regardez vos mains
regardez-les
vous aussi
vous participez du mystère

•

I will die by chance
but no one will choose my grave
in my place

•

Today
the words stretch with ease
and yawn
they have a peach-like complexion

•

In the wings
the comedy
on stage
the tragedy
in the hall
a choice chorus of individual admirers
outside
the rain is falling
on the deserted city

•

Paris
plays
at being Paris

•

There is
more falsity than truth

•

Je mourrai par hasard
mais personne ne choisira ma tombe
à ma place

•

Aujourd'hui
les mots s'étirent d'aise
et bâillent
ils ont un teint de pêche

•

Dans les coulisses
la comédie
sur scène
la tragédie
dans la salle
le chœur d'admirateurs à la carte
dehors
la pluie tombe
sur la ville déserte

•

Paris
joue
à être Paris

•

Il y a
plus de faux que de vrai

because of this the false
costs more

•

Science is needed
to tour the city
without feeling like an alien
and being able to say to the city
how beautiful you are!

•

I'm not dead from having seen Paris

•

If I live better here
it's because I am not
in the race

•

Here
one is always looking for something
in the cafés, churches, squares
and even in the trashcans
we look within the other, in ourselves
in the hubbub of the sidewalks
the calm of bridges
in the stagnant water of fountains
and on indiscrete benches
we look upstairs, downstairs, in front of us for
a metro ticket
a lost land or a lost woman

avec cela que le faux
coûte plus cher

•

Il en faut de la science
pour faire le tour de la ville
sens se sentir étranger
et pouvoir dire à la ville
comme tu es belle !

•

Je ne suis pas mort d'avoir vu Paris

•

Si je vis mieux ici
c'est parce que je ne suis pas
dans la course

•

Ici
on cherche toujours quelque chose
dans les cafés, les églises, les places
et jusque dans les poubelles
on cherche en l'autre, en soi
dans la cohue des trottoirs
l'accalmie des ponts
dans l'eau stagnante des fontaines
et sur les bancs indiscrets
on cherche en bas, en haut, devant soi
un ticket de métro
une terre ou une femme perdues

a book that one will read
on a hospital bed or in prison
a song without title
a solid can opener
a bird that only sings at night
One searches
for a look that will shake up your life
a graffito addressed to you alone
an Arab knocker on an Italian door
a postcard you sent twenty years ago
that the recipient resold
your date of death inscribed
on a tree trunk
in a small park
that you are just crossing
Here
we are always looking for something
on the delirious carousel
of desire

•

Delirium
touches it all
it is a formidable analyst
but the thing is
it does not draw conclusions

•

Did I hurt
my fellow men
my loved ones
my people?
Did I betray anyone?

un livre qu'on lira
sur un lit d'hôpital ou en prison
une chanson sans titre
un ouvre-boîte solide
un oiseau qui ne chante que de nuit
On cherche
un regard qui fera basculer votre vie
un graffiti à vous seul adressé
un heurtoir arabe sur une porte italienne
une carte postale que vous avez envoyé il y a vingt ans
et que le destinataire a revendue
votre date de mort inscrite
sur un tronc d'arbre
dans un petit parc
que vous ne faites que traverser
Ici
on cherche toujours quelque chose
dans le carrousel délirant
du désir

•

Le délire
touche à tout
c'est un redoutable analyste
mais voilà
il ne tire pas de conclusions

•

Ai-je fait mal
à mes semblables
à mes proches
à mon peuple ?
Ai-je trahi quelqu'un ?

I ask these questions
to not insult
the future

•

I have never had anything to sell
A fallen angel
who does not relinquish
I really want to be that

•

It is defeats
which teach us
generosity

•

I do not deny it
writing is a luxury
but it is the only luxury
where man
only exploits himself

•

We believe we are driving the planet
we do nothing
but accompany it

•

The prophet destroys the idols
the tyrant
builds statues

Je pose ces questions
pour ne pas insulter
l'avenir

•

Je n'ai jamais rien eu à vendre
Un ange déchu
qui ne se résigne pas
je veux bien être cela

•

Ce sont les défaites
qui nous apprennent
la générosité

•

Je ne le nie pas
l'écriture est un luxe
mais c'est le seul luxe
où l'homme
n'exploite que lui-même

•

Nous croyons conduire la planète
nous ne faisons
que l'accompagner

•

Le prophète détruit les idoles
le tyran
édifie des statues

•

I know
some diseases
empathize with all the others
but I never understood
the sickness of money
and power
Should I sympathize
with this one too?

•

We also do a great job
finishing off the children
with weapons, with hunger
without bringing about
the apocalypse
without the Savior coming
to stop this madness

•

Do not hold your nose
happy people
give alms
there's always something to take
to take more of
from your legal kidnapping

•

I shock you
because I do not want to be
your equal

•

Je connais
quelque maladies
compatis à toutes les autres
mais je n'ai jamais compris
la maladie de l'argent
et du pouvoir
Dois-je compatir aussi
à celle-ci ?

•

On achève bien aussi
les enfants
par les armes, par la faim
sans que cela provoque
l'apocalypse
sans que le Sauveur accoure
pour arrêter cette folie

•

Ne vous bouchez pas le nez
peuples heureux
faites l'aumône
c'est toujours ça à prendre
à reprendre
de votre rapt légal

•

Je vous choque
parce que je ne veux pas être
votre égal

•

My religion forbids it to me
because you see
I am a believer
as only a true pagan can be
escaped from the inquisitions
which gave the world to be plundered
to the toothless of your species

•

Yet I do not abandon you
I pity you living
I pity you dead
I am your negative blood

•

A short recess
softness is required
to scream death

•

Privileges degrade

•

I do not deserve anything
nothing deserves me
I paid my debt
with gratitude
and ingratitude

•

Ma religion me l'interdit
car voyez-vous
Je suis croyant
comme seul peut l'être un vrai païen
échappé aux inquisitions
qui ont donné le monde en pâture
aux édentés de votre espèce

•

Pourtant je ne vous abandonne pas
je vous plains vivants
je vous plains morts
je suis votre sang négatif

•

Une courte récréation
il y faut de la douceur
pour crier à mort

•

Les privilèges rabaissent

•

Je ne mérite rien
rien ne me mérite
Je suis quitte
avec la gratitude
et l'ingratitude

•

History will judge, they say
Another trial

•

Waiting
is my *bête noire*

•

I open the window
of my secret garden
Predators have ravaged everything
they have even taken
the secret of my garden

•

The farewell
is already a ceremony
of return

•

To return
Did I ever leave?
I always come back
I never leave

•

Intransigence
that is what allows
tolerance

•

L'Histoire jugera, dit-on
Encore un procè !

•

Attendre
c'est ma bête noire

•

J'ouvre la fenêtre
de mon jardin secret
Les prédateurs ont tout saccagé
ils ont emporté
jusqu'au secret de mon jardin

•

L'adieu
C'est déjà une cérémonie
du retour

•

Revenir
Suis-je parti ?
Toujours je reviens
Jamais je ne pars

•

L'intransigeance
c'est cela qui permet
la tolérance

•

Often
I feel diminished
faulty somehow
when I am being congratulated

•

I read a lot
in the smile of others
but I do not know
what mine is made of

•

I condemned my children
to the burden I carry
should I drop it
to free them of it?

•

I worry
when I don't dream anymore

•

There ought to be
a bank of dreams
like the blood banks

•

Souvent
je me sens diminué
fautif quelque part
quand on vient me féliciter

•

Je lis beaucoup
dans le sourire des autres
mais je ne sais pas de quoi est fait
le mien

•

J'ai condamné mes enfants
au fardeau que je porte
dois-je le déposer
pour qu'ils s'en libèrent ?

•

Je suis inquiet
quand je ne rêve plus

•

Il devrait y avoir
une banque du rêve
à l'instar des banques du sang

•

Smiling
cannot be learned
it is a gift

•

I do not expect anything from life
I go
to meet it

•

The bite of days. Fallow love. The quartered horse. Wild ink. The contagious rose. The marbled island. The vomit of the blind. The name of mud. The distracted god. The knowing bullets. The mutilated sheets. The cage of the sky. The white café. The sob of things. The leprosy of the North. The small lakes of the mouth. The common pit of crowns. The nomadic flame. The ashes of words.

•

You can fall in love at first sight
for a word
A word comes your way
and gives you
the key to the work

•

Le sourire
ne s'apprend pas
c'est un don

•

Je n'attends rien de la vie
je vais
à sa rencontre

•

La morsure des jours. L'amour en jachère. Le cheval écartelé. L'encre sauvage. La rose contagieuse. L'île de marbre. Les vomissures de l'aveugle. Le nom de la boue. Le dieu distrait. Les balles savantes. Les draps mutilés. La cage du ciel. Le café blanc. Le sanglot des choses. La lèpre du Nord. Les petits lacs de la bouche. La fosse commune des couronnes. La flamme nomade. La cendre des mots.

•

On peut avoir le coup de foudre
pour un mot
Un mot vient à votre rencontre
et vous tend
la clé de l'œuvre

Contributors

ABDELLATIF LAÂBI is a poet, novelist, playwright, translator, and political activist. He was born in Fez, Morocco, in 1942. In the 1960s, Laâbi was the founding editor of *Souffles-Anfas*, or *Breaths*, a widely influential literary review that was banned in 1972, at which point Laâbi was imprisoned for eight and a half years. Laâbi's accolades include the Prix Goncourt de la Poésie (2009), the Académie Française's Grand Prix de la Francophonie (2011), and the Roger Kowalski Award for Poetry for *Presque riens* (2021). Laâbi's works have been translated into Arabic, Spanish, German, Italian, Dutch, Turkish, and English, and Laâbi himself has translated into French the works of Mahmoud Darwish, Abdul Wahab al-Bayati, Mohammed Al-Maghout, Saâdi Youssef, Abdallah Zrika, Ghassan Kanafani, and Qassim Haddad.

GUILLEMETTE JOHNSTON is a professor of French at DePaul University. A specialist in Rousseau and the French Enlightenment, she has also taught broadly in the areas of French and Francophone literature, as well as Liberal Studies Program focal point courses on the *Yoga Sutra* of Patañjali and the psychology of fairy tales, and DEI sophomore seminars on Race, Power, and Resistance. She has lived in the French Caribbean and Algeria, and has authored a monograph on Frantz Fanon that appeared in the *Dictionary of Literary Biography*. Francophone courses she has taught include sections on Islam and France, Haiti, the shattering of identity by immigration and colonialism, French Canadian literature, the problem of identity in the French Caribbean, and Maghrebi novels of childhood. She is coeditor of *JPSE: Journal for the Philosophical Study of Education*, and a cotranslator (with Allan Johnston) of poems published in *AzonaL, MayDay Magazine, Metamorphoses, Ezra, Transference*, and *Milles Feuilles*. She is the author of *Lectures poétiques: La Représentation poétique du discours théorique chez Jean-Jacques Rousseau* (1996), and has published scholarly articles in *Romanic Review, French Forum, Studies on Voltaire and the Eighteenth Century, Pensée libre, Études Jean-Jacques Rousseau,* the *MLA Approaches to Teaching* series, and elsewhere.

ALLAN JOHNSTON earned his M.A. in Creative Writing and his Ph.D. in English from the University of California, Davis. His poems have appeared in over sixty journals, including *Poetry, Poetry East, Rattle,* and *Rhino*. He has published three full-length poetry collections (*Tasks of Survival,* 1996; *In a Window,* 2018; *Sable and Selected Poems,* 2022) and three chapbooks (*Northport,* 2010; *Departures,* 2013; *Contingencies,* 2015), and has received an Illinois Arts Council Fellowship, Pushcart Prize nominations, and First Prize in Poetry in the Outrider Press Literary Anthology competition. His translations and cotranslations with Guillemette Johnston of poems from the French and German have appeared in *AzonaL, Ezra, MayDay Magazine, Metamorphosis,* and *Transference*. He has taught writing and literature at several colleges and universities, including most recently Columbia College and DePaul University in Chicago. He reads or has read for *Word River, r.kv.r.y,* and the Illinois Emerging Poets competition, and is coeditor of *JPSE: Journal for the Philosophical Study of Education*. His scholarly articles have appeared in *Twentieth Century Literature, College Literature,* and several other journals.

Shanti Arts

Nature · Art · Spirit

Please visit us online
to browse our entire book catalog,
including poetry collections and fiction,
books on travel, nature, healing, art,
photography, and more.

Also take a look at our highly regarded art
and literary journal, *Still Point Arts Quarterly*,
which may be downloaded for free.

www.shantiarts.com

www.ingramcontent.com/pod-product-compliance
Lightning Source LLC
Chambersburg PA
CBHW050517170426
43201CB00013B/1993